Too Many Pastors?

Too Many Pastors?

THE
CLERGY JOB MARKET

Jackson W. Carroll
Robert L. Wilson

The Pilgrim Press
New York

Library of Congress Cataloging in Publication Data

Carroll, Jackson W
  Too many pastors?

  Includes bibliographical references.
  1. Clergy—United States.   2. Protestant churches
—United States. 3. Labor supply—United States.
I. Wilson, Robert Leroy, 1925-   joint author.
III. Title.
BR517.C33   331.12'91253'0973   80-16037
ISBN 0-8298-0405-6 (pbk.)

The scripture references in the book are from the *Revised Standard Version of the Bible,* copyright 1946, 1952 and © 1971 by the Division of Christian Education, National Council of Churches, and are used by permission.

The Pilgrim Press, 132 West 31 Street, New York, New York 10001

To

Anne and Betty

whose assistance, patience,
and understanding
provided necessary and loving support in
the making of this book

Contents

Notes   167

Foreword

It is only a slight exaggeration to suggest that the church building boom of the 1950s reinforced and gave physical expression to the belief that the purpose of the Christian congregation could be summarized in three words: worship, education, and fellowship. Those three words summarized the basic components of thousands of long-range construction programs.

As we move into a new decade it appears those three words have been replaced by a new trinity. If one takes seriously what is written and spoken, the operational definition of the reasons for existence of the worshiping congregation gradually has evolved into a new threefold statement of purpose: provide a ministry of Word and Sacrament, own and maintain an adequate meeting place, and provide employment for the clergy.

The growing assumption that there will be an offstreet parking space at the end of every automobile journey and the rapidly escalating charges for utility services have combined to make the cost of owning and maintaining its own separate meeting house a source of anxiety for thousands of congregations, both urban and rural. That issue tops the agenda for the trustees of many congregations.

From the ministerial and denominational perspective, the pressure to provide satisfying employment for an excessive number of ordained ministers and seminary graduates has become a major concern. This excellent book by two highly skilled and veteran observers of the Protestant church scene in the United States offers the first comprehensive, informed, and interpretative analysis of the subject. Their analysis is based on a study of the supply and demand for ministers in a dozen American denominations, and it both reviews the origins of the problem and suggests some creative responses.

This is a subject that is highly vulnerable to oversimplification. Some denominational leaders contend, "The real problem is not a surplus of ministers; it is a shortage of really competent and committed pastors." Others argue, "The basic problem is that inflation and escalating costs have forced many churches that once had their own full-time resident minister to go to a part-time pastor." A few insist, "The heart of the problem is that too many ministers look forward to serving a larger congregation by moving, rather than by building up the church they are now serving." Some lay leaders, and especially those in small churches, ask, "What's wrong? Why don't the seminaries turn out ministers who want to preach because they love the Lord, rather than for love of the dollar? If there is a surplus of ministers, how come we've been without a regular preacher for nearly three years? We've interviewed at least a dozen, but each one wants more money than we can pay!" Those who have examined the seminary graduation figures for several decades may be inclined to suggest, "This is only a temporary phenomenon due to the low number of retirements during the late 1970s and early 1980s. Very few people entered the ministry during the Great Depression, so today we have very few retiring and thus few vacancies. Wait until we are hit by the flood of retirements of those who graduated from seminary in the 1945-54 era. When that wave hits us, we'll have another shortage!" Each of these statements reflects one facet of reality, but each one also greatly oversimplifies the issue.

There are many, many factors that have combined to produce the oversupply of clergy. This list includes the fact that the costs of providing person-centered and labor-intensive services (such as education, hospital care, and pastoral services) have risen far more rapidly than have family incomes. For example, the average cost for one patient for one day in a community hospital in 1950 was $8, or approximately two thirds of a day's wages for the average manufacturing worker. By 1978 the average cost for one patient for one day in the hospital was $187, or more than triple a day's wages for the average manufacturing worker. While ministers' salaries have gone up at a relatively moderate pace, many congregations that could afford full-time resident pastors back during the Great Depression found themselves priced out of the ministerial market-place during the post-World War II era.

12

One of the less visible, but very significant background factors behind the current oversupply of clergy has been the gradual drift of the laity toward larger churches. Today a general rule of thumb is that in many denominations 8 percent of the congregations include one third of the members. In some, such as the Presbyterian Church in the U.S., slightly fewer than 6 percent of all congregations account for one third of the communicant members. It is not uncommon for a 200- or 300-member congregation to be served by a full-time resident minister, but it is very unusual for the 1,200-member congregation to have a staff of four to six ordained ministers. The greater the concentration of members in large congregations, the lower the demand for ministers.

One of the more subtle, but frequently neglected factors that Carroll and Wilson lift up can be described as "careerism." Back in the first half of the eighteenth century the average tenure of the Congregational minister in New England was approximately twenty-eight years.[1] Most served only one congregation during their entire ministerial career. A similar pattern prevailed in several denominations during the nineteenth century and well into the first half of this century. It is not unusual, for example, to find a Lutheran parish that had been served by only three or four pastors between 1850 and 1950.

In recent years, however, that pattern has changed, and an increasing number of ministers expect to move after only five to ten years in the same parish. This tendency is easier to accommodate in a closed placement system, such as The United Methodist Church, than in the open placement systems. In most Protestant denominations the mobility of the clergy is inhibited unless there is a substantial number of vacant pulpits. The increased supply of ministers has reduced the number of vacancies in congregations with at least 300 members and paying a cash salary (in 1980 dollars) of $12,000 or more. Thus the pressures of the oversupply of ministers are enhanced by the contemporary emphasis on careerism.[2]

Additional factors that may make this volume of even greater relevance for pastors and denominational leaders of 1989 than of 1981 are (1) inflation, (2) improved health care, (3) pressures to raise the age of retirement, and (4) the limitations of denominational pensions. In the past years death, disability, and retirement created a

13

predictable number of retirements every year. Now, as a result of the longest inflationary cycle in American history, many retirees are finding themselves in serious financial difficulties. Retirement is no longer the attractive option at age sixty-five that it once was. Furthermore, illnesses and accidents that produced a retirement because of disability in 1955 now can be treated by advanced medical skills to produce several more years of productive service. The basic signs suggest that many ministers may choose, and others will be forced by financial pressures, to defer retirement until age sixty-eight or seventy or seventy-two. This will add to the pressures of the oversupply. A simple thing such as the reduction in the national speed limit to fifty-five miles per hour has also probably eliminated several dozen vacancies that otherwise would have occurred.

In addition, inflation has had a serious impact on denominational receipts. This inevitably will mean a decrease in the amount of denominational subsidies available to enable the smaller congregations to be served by full-time ministers. The decrease in the financial resources of denominational agencies already has intensified the pressures of oversupply by the elimination of scores of denominational positions for clergy.

Finally, mention must be made of the baby boom of the 1956-61 era. These were the only years in American history when the number of babies born each year exceeded 4.2 million. If the seminaries attract their traditional share of each age cohort, and if the typical seminary graduate is in the twenty-four to twenty-eight age bracket, this will mean record numbers of seminary graduates entering the ministerial marketplace during the 1980-89 period. Their numbers will more than offset the anticipated increase in the number of retirements of the seminary graduates of the post-World War II decade. Thus far it appears that a substantial number of the new entrants into the ministerial marketplace will be (1) women from the theologically more liberal denominational seminaries and (2) men from the "transdenominational" seminaries, such as Gordon-Conwell, Fuller, Trinity, Asbury, Oral Roberts University, and others. That combination will make the placement process even more interesting.

In other words, the placement crunch may become more severe during this new decade, and this timely book may become an

14

increasingly valuable tool in understanding the nature of this issue and the alternative responses open to ministers, denominational leaders, and congregations.

Lyle E. Schaller
Yokefellow Institute

Introduction

A cartoon pictures a young man wearing a clerical collar looking at a sign tacked on the door of a Gothic-style church building. The sign reads, in bold letters: NO HELP WANTED!

Although the cartoon is not an entirely accurate reflection of Protestantism today, the employment situation for clergy is radically different from that of the 1950s and early 1960s. Gone are the days when denominational leaders wondered aloud where they were going to find enough pastors to fill the vacant pulpits; when they lamented that too many ordained persons were going into nonparish positions; when the theological seminaries were criticized because too many graduates did not want to be pastors of congregations; and when there was great anguish over anyone leaving the ministry. Now church leaders worry about having more ordained persons than positions for them to fill, are concerned that the clergy now employed in nonparish positions may want to become pastors of local churches, and fear that the seminaries may be preparing too many persons for ordained ministry.

In one sense an oversupply of clergy is a contradiction in terms. If a minister is defined as someone who is dedicated to and prepared for service in the name of Christ, there can never be too many. However, some denominations find themselves in the position of having more ordained persons than there are congregations that can afford to employ them. A surplus of ministers, as the term is used in this book, is an imbalance between available clergy and the number of positions for them to occupy. In this sense an oversupply of clergy (or an undersupply of appropriate positions) existed in a number of denominations in the late 1970s and will likely continue in the early 1980s.

A surplus of ordained ministers is a painful and embarrassing situation for the church—much more so than a shortage. A shortage tends to occur during a period of expansion and growth; a surplus tends to come at a time of decline and retrenchment. For the church to have to tell young persons who have been recruited and trained for ordained ministry that there may be no positions for them is embarrassing.

This book is about the oversupply of clergy, why it has occurred, and what can be done about it. The first part describes the situation and deals with why there is a surplus of ministers. The second section discusses the consequences for clergy, congregations, and denominations. The third part considers what ministers, congregations, denominations, and theological seminaries can do to cope with the situation.

While an attempt has been made to approach the subject with the objectivity of social scientists, we, the authors, are also ordained ministers, with experience as pastors, teachers, and researchers. Our perspective is that of persons who are within the church and committed to its ministry and mission.

This book is based on research on the clergy employment situation conducted by The Hartford Seminary Foundation, with grant support from the Lilly Endowment, Inc. Twelve denominations were studied. These were selected to provide diversity in types of polity, theology, denominational size, and geography. Denominations included are the American Baptist Churches in the U.S.A., Christian Church (Disciples of Christ), Church of God (Anderson, Indiana), Church of the Nazarene, The Episcopal Church, Lutheran Church in America, Presbyterian Church in the U.S., Reformed Church in America, Southern Baptist Convention, United Church of Christ, The United Methodist Church, and The United Presbyterian Church in the U.S.A. The following data was gathered and analyzed:

1. Statistical trends in each of the denominations, from 1950 to the present, including the number of clergy, congregations, and church members
2. Information on the deployment and age distribution of the clergy
3. Over two hundred interviews with denominational officials on both the national and regional judicatory level
4. Visitations to twenty-five theological seminaries; adminis-

trators, recruitment and placement officers, and four to eight students interviewed at each

5. Questionnaires distributed to a 10 percent random sample of first- and third-year students in preordination degree programs at representative denominational and independent schools of theology to determine the students' perspectives on the clergy job market

6. Studies of clergy placement and deployment, and of ministers' attitudes concerning the job situation, conducted by the denominations and others.

An earlier report summarized in full the data that was gathered.[1] Here we present only a limited number of tables in the body of the text, concentrating instead on the consequences of the job situation for clergy and others affected and on strategies for responding to the situation. Additional tables from the earlier report are included in the Appendix and reference is made to them where appropriate in the text.

This study was made possible by the combined efforts of many people. We are indebted to the Lilly Endowment, Inc. for funding the project, and to The Hartford Seminary Foundation, Duke University Divinity School, and our colleagues in these institutions for support and constructive criticism provided during the project. An advisory committee consisting of Yorke Allen Jr., Joan B. Bowman, Frank R.L. Egloff, James Gunn, Nathanael Guptill, Loyde Hartley, Neeley McCarter, Marnie W. Mueller, Roddey Reid Jr., David S. Schuller, Joseph Wagner, Barbara Wheeler, and Elliott Wright met twice for two-day sessions to contribute valuable critique and insights. Denominational and seminary officials provided access to church records, assisted with other data gathering, and gave the time to be interviewed. Further important insights were given by the denominational executives of the Professional Church Leadership group of the National Council of Churches. The data was presented to church leaders and seminary officials at three consultations. Consultation participants provided critique based on their experience and gave suggestions for types of responses, many of which are included in the following chapters.

Although it would be impossible to mention individually all those who helped with the study, several need special acknowledgment. Anne Carroll spent many tedious hours searching out and summarizing statistical data, and managing other aspects of the data-gathering process. David Roozen assisted with computer programming and data analysis; Amy Beveridge, Anne Daniels, and Gilda Simpson provided secretarial assistance. Edgar Mills and Robert Bonn made available data from the clergy support studies of 1963, 1968, and 1973.

It is our hope that these findings will be of help to the clergy, the local congregations, and the denominations, as they attempt to plan for the leadership needs of the churches in the period ahead.

Part 1

The Present Predicament

Chapter I

Encountering the Clergy Job Market

I don't really have to leave St. Paul's, but I have been here almost ten years and I think it's time to move on. I feel I'm ready to handle a larger congregation. So far all I've found are similar or smaller congregations. I guess I'll stay put, and wait for something to open up.

—Protestant pastor

An encounter with the job market can be a traumatic experience, regardless of one's occupation. So much of an individual's identity and feelings of self-worth are bound up with her or his job. Many jobs, especially professional occupations, are viewed as callings, a situation symbolized by the easy interchangeability of the words vocation (from the Latin *vocare,* to call) and job. Clergy in particular understand themselves to have a calling from God. Thus when they encounter the job market, through which they seek avenues to respond to their divine calling, there is a special sense of concern that may or may not be present for the person seeking a position in a bank or a manufacturing plant. "Is it possible," the clergyperson asks, "for me to find an appropriate way of fulfilling God's call to the ministry?"

This chapter presents several case histories to illustrate the experiences some ministers have had with the job market. Each case is based on actual experiences; however, names have been changed to protect the identity of the persons involved.

SEARCHING FOR A FIRST POSITION

John is thirty-one, married, and the father of two children. After college he went into the dry cleaning business. He was fairly successful; his business was prospering to the point of opening several branch stores, and he and his family were comfortably settled in a new home in an attractive suburb. "Despite the fact that everything was going well, I wasn't satisfied," he commented. "I suppose that in the back of my mind I had always considered the clergy but never did anything about it."

At age twenty-nine John did something about it: he sold his business and entered seminary to prepare for the priesthood in The Episcopal Church. His wife is completely in agreement with his decision, and she has been working part time while he is in school. Now he is in his senior year and beginning to look for a parish. "I really would like to return to my home diocese, because that is where our roots are. Both our families are there," he observed. However, conversations with his bishop have not been encouraging. The job situation is very tight in his diocese; there are no current vacancies in parishes that can afford a full-time priest, and few vacancies are anticipated in the next few years.

When asked about options, he replied, "I understand there are openings in parishes in Nebraska. If I can't return to my home diocese, I'll try Nebraska." He went on, "The Anglican Church of Canada will accept our training, and they need priests. If I can't get a parish in the United States, I'll go to Canada."

When asked if he would consider securing a secular job and serving as a part-time clergyman, he replied with some determination, "I came to seminary to become a full-time parish priest; I intend to reach that goal." For John, there is no other option at this time.

THE MINISTER IS A WOMAN

Approximately two decades ago, when she was a young adult, Betty seriously considered entering some type of Christian vocation. Marriage altered her plans. Two years after she married her husband was stricken with multiple sclerosis, which resulted in his being an invalid until his death, thirteen years later. With an ill husband and a young daughter to support, Betty returned to work, taking a management position with a utility company. After her husband's death she again considered full-time Christian service but was reluctant to give up her job and embark on a new career. She commented, "The Lord was calling me to preach, but I was resisting. My health was affected, and I spent some time in the university hospital undergoing extensive tests. Finally, when the basement in my house caved in, I decided that the Lord was trying to tell me something!"

Betty consulted with a United Methodist district superintendent, who encouraged her to begin the necessary preparation for the ministry. "He helped me fill out the application for the Ministerial Course of Study school and mailed it himself, because he said he was afraid I might change my mind." (The Ministerial Course of Study is a United Methodist, five-year summer program for persons entering the ministry who are at an age when it is impossible to attend seminary.) She studied the required courses for the next two summers, while retaining her position with the utility company. At this point the district superintendent arranged for Betty to be appointed pastor of five small rural churches; their congregations ranged in size from 25 to 110. At the age of thirty-five, with a teenage daughter, she began her ministerial career with "the feeling that I was doing the right thing but with a lot of anxiety."

She has been pastor of these five churches for over three years. When she first arrived there was some opposition. One laywoman announced that she agreed with Paul concerning women in the church and would not attend church until a man was appointed. This person has since changed her mind; Betty's pastoral care of the laywoman's invalid mother has turned an opponent into a supporter and friend.

Betty is the first woman minister of any denomination to serve in that county. She reports that she is well accepted by both church members and ministerial colleagues. Her churches are prospering. She is happy serving a five-point circuit and anticipates no problem in securing another, perhaps similar, appointment when the time comes for her to move. Recently, a member told her, "We hope you will stay and be our pastor until you retire." Betty's reply was, "I'd like to stay as long as my ministry is effective."

THE PAINS OF TERMINATION

George has been pastor of a Presbyterian church for eleven years and would consider his ministry effective during this time. The congregation has remained stable in a period when the denomination has been losing members. He has been particularly interested in social service activities for certain disadvantaged groups in the community and has been instrumental in initiating several such programs.

A small but active group of laypersons became increasingly opposed to George. The reasons are hard to pinpoint, but they seem to be a combination of theological differences and personality clashes. Some felt he was spending too much time in community service activities. These persons secured a majority on the governing board and began to urge George to resign. The relationship between the minister and a portion of the congregation deteriorated to the point that it was agreed the minister would take a three months' leave of absence. The assumption was that this would be a cooling-off period, after which George would return. At the end of three months it was obvious that he couldn't return as pastor. Thus the relationship was terminated. The denomination has arranged for a retired pastor who lives in a nearby city to supply the pulpit.

George and his family continue to live in the parsonage while he searches for another church. To date he's had interviews with several congregations but hasn't received a call. Because of the conflict with his previous congregation, some churches may be reluctant to call him. He feels that his ministry has been successful, and that he should be able to secure a call to a church commensurate with his experience and ability. In the meantime he has secured a clerical position with a business, which he regards as temporary. As time passes, George and his wife are growing disillusioned with their denomination's placement process—one in which they see themselves as victims. They cannot occupy the parsonage indefinitely. The period of transition has continued longer than they expected, and the outcome is still in doubt.

THE CLERGY COUPLE

Sue and Paul met each other when they were students in seminary. Both were United Methodists but from different sections of the country, and hence from different annual conferences. Sue had decided to enter the ministry after two years of public school teaching; Paul entered seminary a year later. They were married when Sue graduated; at the time, Paul still had another year of school to complete.

After their marriage Paul secured a student pastorate, from which he commuted to school. Sue took extra courses and for a brief time served as interim pastor of a small congregation. Both Paul and Sue had been ordained deacons (the first step in the United Methodist ordination process) and had been received as probationary members of their home annual conferences. The problem was that their affiliations were with different annual conferences.

When Sue asked for a transfer to the annual conference where her husband was a member and where she was living, the request was denied. The experience was disconcerting, because in effect it meant that under the United Methodist polity she would either have to return to her annual conference and receive an appointment or give up her ministerial status. Paul reports that "Sue was terribly upset by the rejection."

At this point she secured a position as director of education on the staff of a large congregation in a nearby city. Meanwhile, Paul graduated and continued as pastor of the church he had served as a student.

Sue asked again to transfer to Paul's annual conference and was again rejected. She pointed out that she already had a job in a church and could be appointed minister of education. The bishop suggested that some arrangement might be made by which she retained her affiliation with her home conference but continued in her church staff job as minister of education. There was serious question as to whether or not denominational polity would permit this. The issue was resolved when a man who was a member of Paul's conference requested to transfer to the one of which Sue was a member. The bishops in effect swapped ministers, with each getting a clergy couple. Sue has since been fully ordained.

Paul continues to serve the same congregation, and Sue is still the minister of education at the same city church. They are uncertain about their future but would prefer an assignment where they could work together rather than in separate jobs. Currently, United

Methodist polity prohibits a clergy couple from sharing a single salary; each must receive the required minimum compensation.

The experience of Paul and Sue illustrates the placement problems of many United Methodist clergy couples. Understandably, they want to serve together. The bishop, who is required by Methodist polity to appoint every minister, is aware that he and his successors could be responsible for placing Paul and Sue for the next forty years. Thus he has been somewhat reluctant to make that commitment, since meshing two careers that may proceed at different paces is difficult. For the time being, Sue and Paul have satisfactory positions, but it is likely that difficulties related to their subsequent assignments will continue.

A "TENTMAKER" MINISTER

Since 1976 Richard, now in his late fifties, has been a "tentmaker," or dual-role, minister. That is, he has worked full time in a secular job, while also carrying out a full ministry as pastor of a small United Presbyterian congregation. The secular job has taken approximately thirty-five hours per week, while the pastorate has required an additional twenty-four. Before engaging in this dual-role style of ministry, Richard spent twenty years as a full-time pastor; the last seven of these years he was senior pastor of a 1,500-member urban congregation.

What led Richard to this change? Several factors were operative. For one thing, over the years he had become more and more uncomfortable with the idea that, in his status as full-time pastor, he was financially dependent on his congregation. Another element was his dissatisfaction with his role in the church; he did not feel that he was using his capabilities to the fullest. At the same time, however, he perceived that he had probably gone as high up the career ladder as he would be able to go, and that he would have another seventeen years of ministry at this level if he chose to remain in a full-time position. Further, there were times when he had doubts about his credibility with the business people to whom he ministered. Also, he was aware that many small churches had a need for clergy leadership but were unable to afford it on a full-time basis. The influence of these factors coalesced with the initiation of an experimental program to assist clergy who wanted to try dual-role ministries. Richard enrolled in the program, and his experience thus far has been mixed but essentially positive.

After extensive testing, and coaching in job-seeking, Richard began searching for a secular job that would be compatible with a call to a small congregation, which he was also seeking. A number of job applications ended in rejection. He was thought to be overqualified. Finally, at the same time he was offered a position as administrator of a mental health program, he was called as pastor of a small congregation. A contract recognizing his dual-role status and the mutual obligations of both pastor and people in such a situation was carefully negotiated with the congregation.

The arrangement with the church has worked quite well. The congregation has been quite pleased to have the services of a person of Richard's ability, although at first they apologized for not being able to afford him full time. The laity have assumed more responsibility in the ministry of the church. Richard has found the arrangement fulfilling but quite demanding. His secular job also gave him satisfaction, although a political struggle brought about his resignation from the mental health agency. Subsequently, he has secured a job as a telephone representative for a health insurance company, which he finds "very satisfying. It has limited responsibility, uses my counseling skills, has regular hours (forty per week), and leaves me with more energy for church work than the mental health agency did."

Richard continues to be optimistic about his dual-role ministry. "I know the dual-role is a success," he says, "because I go to committee meetings and come home with nothing to do. The laypeople accept all the responsibilities. They are now asking for lay pastoral care training!"

A SUCCESSFUL SEARCH FOR A CHANGE OF CHURCHES

There is a variation in the way clergy experience the job market. Not everyone finds it difficult to secure a call. Andy is an example. He has recently begun serving a suburban United Church of Christ congregation of just over one thousand members. Even though he's only in his midthirties, it's his third parish since graduating from seminary, twelve years ago.

As Andy was completing his eighth year in his previous parish, he felt himself at a turning point regarding his career. His ministry had been an effective one, and he had assumed various leadership roles in the community and the denomination. There was no pressure from within the parish for him to make a change, nor was he unhappy in the situation. Also, his wife had a good job that provided fulfillment for her and supplemented their income. The problem was, as he put it, he "felt *too* comfortable." Several major long-term projects in the parish had been brought to completion, and Andy had to decide whether to stay on and initiate new ministries or to make a change. He chose the latter.

The difficult job situation for clergy was well known to him. Therefore, when he updated his employment dossier, or profile, with the United Church of Christ Office for Church Life and Leadership, so that it would be sent to vacant churches, he fully expected a long wait—as much as two years. Such an expectation was further warranted because he had restricted his choice of possible locations to three UCC conferences. Andy talked personally with the conference minister in each of the three conferences of his choice. Each warned him of the tight job situation and encouraged him not to expect a quick response.

Both his and their expectations of a long wait proved wrong. Within two months of activating his profile he had engaged in interviews with five large parishes, three of which almost simultaneously extended calls to him. Four of these committees invited him to candidate, that is, to preach a sermon before the congregation and to be presented to them as the committee's nominee. How did he feel about the situation? "It was a good ego trip," he remarked, "but I got over that quickly. Frankly, it was almost too much to handle. I had not expected anything like it." When asked how, if at all, his success had affected his relationships with fellow clergy, he said that he had experienced some envy, particularly from older clergy who had been having real difficulty making a change.

What were important factors in Andy's success? While he modestly attributes it to luck, others—including both his present and former conference ministers—view it as a combination of several factors. First is his demonstrated competence in a variety of ministry functions. Second is his age: old enough to have had significant pastoral experience but young enough to have a substantial number of years before retirement. Third, he has a happy, intact marriage with an able, attractive wife. Finally, he received strong personal endorsement from the conference ministers circulating his profile to search committees. The combination of these factors apparently makes his experience somewhat atypical in a time of limited mobility.

AGE AND THE JOB MARKET

Ageism—discrimination against persons on the basis of their age—has joined racism and sexism as an area in which oppression is experienced. While older clergy, especially those in their late fifties, have typically experienced more difficulty in changing jobs than younger clergy, it is harder than ever in today's tight job market.

Take Jim's case. Not only is Jim in the older-clergy age category—he's fifty-seven—he's also divorced and remarried. The combination of these two factors made his attempts to secure a new call within the United Church of Christ a long and often painful process.

Jim's age and the divorce seem to have been the main causes of his problem. It was clearly not a case of being judged ineffective or of lacking experience. Before his divorce Jim had served in several of the largest churches in his conference, and his ministry in them had been distinguished. Additionally, he had served in various leadership capacities in denominational and community affairs.

His divorce, while deeply painful, had resulted from a growing and irreconcilable incompatibility between himself and his wife and not from any act of moral failure. Following the divorce he resigned from his parish and subsequently accepted a call to two small churches, which he served for four years. During this time he met and married a member of one of these churches. It is, from all appearances, a very happy marriage.

In 1975 Jim decided to look for a new call. A conference official encouraged him to "get back into the mainstream of the church," that is, in a larger church rather than the two small congregations he was then serving. Initially, Jim wanted to look primarily in his home conference.

For one and a half years he did not receive a single invitation to be interviewed by a search committee, even though he was strongly endorsed by conference officials. While he did not panic, he tried to find out what was wrong. He was assured that his age and divorce were not at issue. But his doubts about this were growing.

He extended his search to other conferences and finally sparked some interest. Two churches in neighboring conferences invited him for interviews. The first came more than eighteen months after he had begun his job search. Neither of these interviews proved successful, and he did not receive feedback from the churches as to why this was the case. He believes, however, that his age and the divorce were the drawbacks. In the interviews he was candid in discussing the divorce. These two failures left him "deeply disappointed and up in the air."

Then two additional invitations to interview came from churches in other conferences. Unlike the first two, both these interviews proved successful; Jim was invited by each church to be a candidate. While his age and divorce were openly acknowledged, neither proved to be a stumbling block. He chose to accept the call to the smaller of the two churches. Although it is not quite what he had hoped for when he began his search, it is a strong congregation that has received him and his family gladly. For Jim, the entire process took two and a half years—a rather long time from the perspective of one who has only a few years left until retirement. Jim comments, with tongue in cheek, that he has come to believe that "in the United Church of Christ, the years of effective ministry are between the ages thirty-five and forty."

These seven cases by no means constitute a sample of clergy experiencing the job market. They do, however, provide brief glimpses into the situation faced by many clergy, and they are suggestive of some ways in which the differing personal and social characteristics of the clergy affect their job market experiences. While our encounter with these clergy has been limited, their personal struggles will perhaps remain in our consciousness as we turn to the statistics of the clergy job market.

Chapter 2

More Called Than Chosen

The case studies in chapter 1 present the human dimensions in the job market for clergy. They keep before us the real people, their joys and pain, who experience the market forces and are the primary focus of this book. But to understand their situation we need to step back and look more generally at some aspects of the current clergy job market. In this chapter we take an overview of several characteristics of the clergy job market in the denominations chosen for study. While we note variations, we concentrate on characteristics common to most denominations in the 1970s and early 1980s. In chapter 3, we discuss why the situation has occurred at this time. Our summary is primarily nonstatistical; however, as noted previously, it is based on extensive analysis of available denominational statistics and on interviews with denominational officials. Before proceeding, however, a brief note on how clergy are deployed is needed.

METHODS OF DEPLOYING CLERGY

The first method of deploying clergy is one that is completely open. The congregation is free to secure and employ whomever it wishes to have as pastor. The person selected is ordained (certified) by the congregation. The candidate is free to negotiate whatever terms he or she chooses and to accept or reject any offer the congregation may make. The adequacy of the candidate's professional training is determined by the congregation.

Denominations in our study that have an open method include the two Baptist bodies, the Church of God (Anderson, Indiana), Christian Church (Disciples of Christ), and the United Church of Christ. A

Baptist church, for example, may call anyone it desires. The person need not be a Baptist—simply someone who meets the requirements of the congregation. Many Southern Baptist churches resist any attempt by the denomination to develop regional or national deployment practices that might deny local congregations full autonomy of operation. UCC congregations are also free to call any pastor they wish; however, a pastor may be denied standing (formal recognition) by the regional judicatory if he or she fails to meet denominational expectations. There is also a denominationwide office to provide information about vacant pulpits and about pastors seeking a call.

A second method, the restricted open, is similar to the open, with certain modifications. This method is used by such denominations as the two Presbyterian bodies, The Episcopal Church, various Lutheran groups, the Church of the Nazarene, and the Reformed Church in America. In the restricted open method the congregation is still free to call its pastor, but it can only consider persons who have been duly certified as eligible by the appropriate judicatory (for example, the synod or presbytery). In these bodies the denomination determines who is admitted into the ordained ministry. This group decides if the candidate's training is adequate and if her or his theology is appropriately orthodox for the communion. While laypersons may be involved in the process of examination, the clergy tend to determine who will gain entrance into the profession.

A third method by which a congregation secures a pastor can be classified as closed. In American Protestantism this is represented by The United Methodist Church and several other denominations with roots in the Methodist tradition. In a closed method the denominational body has complete control over who is admitted into the ordained ministry. Only the clergy determine which candidates shall be accepted into membership of a United Methodist annual conference and shall be ordained. Once a candidate is admitted (after a probationary period), he or she is guaranteed an appointment as pastor of a congregation or to some other church position. This method operates like a closed shop union, with each member being assured a job.

Ministers are appointed to churches by the bishop. The committee in the local congregation is only advisory. While the bishop will usually attempt to meet the expectations of both congregation and minister (bishops are required to consult with the minister and the local church), the authority to appoint a pastor to a church is the bishop's alone.

In subsequent chapters we consider some of the consequences of these three methods of deploying clergy for imbalances in clergy supply and demand. First, however, we describe characteristics of the current imbalance.

TRENDS IN MEMBERS, CHURCH, AND CLERGY

The majority of active clergy (nonretired) are employed by local churches as pastors or in other professional staff positions. How many clergy a local church employs full time is determined to a considerable degree by the number of members it has. Thus there should be relationship between the number of members and the demand for clergy, and likewise in the number of churches and the demand for clergy. These are not simple relationships. Many clergy do not function in local church settings. Nevertheless, examining the relationship between church membership, the number of churches, and the number of clergy provides a crude indication of any changes in the relationship between the supply and demand for clergy.

We show these relationships in Table 1 (see page 36) as ratios of church members to the total number of clergy in each denomination. Also, we show the ratio of clergy to the number of churches. The ratios are provided for two points in time, 1950 and 1977.[1] Figures for 1977 are the most recent available at the time of this writing. This time period covers both the postwar religious revival, which saw booming membership growth, and new church development in all the denominations through the early 1960s. It also covers the declines in membership and church development that have been experienced by most of the denominations studied since the mid-1960s. Additional data reflecting these trends is shown in the Appendix, Table 3.

In all but two denominations (Church of God and Church of the Nazarene) the ratio of church members to clergy declined over the twenty-seven-year period. This was true whether church membership grew, as it did through the mid-1960s, or declined, as it has

Table 1   Ratios of Church Members to Total Clergy and
of Clergy Per Church, 1950 and 1977,
Selected Denominations

Denominations:	Ratio of Members[a] to Clergy		Ratio of Clergy[b] to Churches	
	1950	1977	1950	1977
American Baptist Churches	251.8	180.0	0.8	1.2
Church of God (Anderson)	43.7	56.9	0.8	1.3
Church of the Nazarene	49.8	60.9	1.3	1.6
Disciples of Christ	215.4	190.5	1.1	1.5
Episcopal Church	373.5	229.1	0.9	1.7
Lutheran Church in America	507.8[c]	381.5	0.9[c]	1.3
Presbyterian Church, U.S.	251.3[c]	167.7	0.8[c]	1.3
Reformed Church in America	320.7	236.3	1.2	1.7
Southern Baptist Convention	317.6	235.6	0.8	1.6
United Church of Christ	239.1[c]	183.4	1.0[c]	1.5
United Methodist Church	353.4[c]	273.5	0.6[c]	0.9
United Presbyterian Church, U.S.A.	260.6	185.3	1.1	1.6

[a]Inclusive membership
[b]Total clergy, including retired
[c]1951 data

Source: <u>Yearbook of American and Canadian Churches</u>, 1951, 1979

since that time. On the average each clergyperson was serving fewer members in 1977 than in 1950. The number of church members necessary to support the full salary of a clergyperson is an important issue about which there is little consensus. However, for many denominations 200 members is a rough rule of thumb. Immediately there are exceptions, such as Church of God and Church of the Nazarene, where per capita giving is quite high and clergy salaries are somewhat lower, lowering the number of members needed to support full-time clergy. Nevertheless, using the figure of 200 members per clergy, it is clear that several denominations cited in Table 1 are approaching or have passed below this mark.

The other ratio in Table 1, the ratio of clergy to churches, reveals a trend toward more clergy per church in all denominations. In 1950 only five of the twelve denominations had more clergy than churches. By 1977 this was true for all but The United Methodist Church.

As we come closer to the end of this century, it has become fashionable to project likely trends for the year 2000. When such projections are based on straight-line extrapolations from past trends, they are highly suspect. Too much can happen, often unanticipated, for such projections to come true. Yet straight-line projections serve two functions. They call attention rather dramatically to the importance and direction of past trends, and they alert us to changes that must be made if we do not want trends of the past to continue into the future. With this as a rationale, we used the trends for the past quarter century to make straight-line projections for the year 2000. These projections are summarized in Table 2. Again, we do not expect these projections to become facts; they are presented to serve the two functions mentioned above.

Table 2 Straight-line Projections for the Year 2000
of the Ratio of Church Members to Clergy and Clergy to Churches
for Selected Denominations

Denominations:	Members to Clergy in 2000	Clergy to Churches in 2000
Church of God (Anderson)	60.1	1.6
Church of the Nazarene	73.4	1.8
Disciples of Christ	88.2	2.5
Episcopal Church	31.1	2.5
Lutheran Church in America	238.4	2.0
Presbyterian Church, U.S.	53.8	2.0
Reformed Church in America	163.3	2.2
Southern Baptist Convention	111.8	2.6
United Church of Christ	78.2	2.1
United Methodist Church	218.2	1.0
United Presbyterian Church, U.S.A.	65.4	2.1

The straight-line projections for 2000, when compared with the actual trends since 1950, further emphasize the considerable changes that occurred between 1950 and 1977, especially in the ratio of church members to clergy. Indeed, if the trends were actually to continue as they have from 1950 to the present, a few denominations would reach a ratio of one member per clergy in only a few years beyond 2000. For example, this would be the case in The Episcopal Church by 2004 and in two Presbyterian bodies by 2011 and 2012. Such an unlikely occurrence would provide the possibility of a rather full ministry to members, to say the least! The other projection, clergy per church, shows an increase in most denominations of two clergy per church by the year 2000.

The overall implication of these tables is that the number of church members and the number of local congregations have not kept pace with the number of clergy. This is particularly true since the mid to late 1960s. It suggests that there has been a decline in an important source of demand, while the supply of clergy has grown.

TYPES OF CLERGY POSITIONS

Only part of the demand for clergy comes from local congregations. Clergy are employed in a variety of nonparish positions within the church system and in other religious agencies, and these have increased over the years. Sociologist Gibson Winter has documented the formalization of denominations that brought large increases in positions—presumably filled mostly by clergy—in denominational bureaucracies. In the Disciples of Christ, for example, the number of national administrative positions increased tenfold, from sixteen in 1900 to 162 in 1962.[2] Furthermore, clergy are frequently employed in secular occupations while continuing to hold ecclesiastical credentials. Such clergy are potentially available for church-related positions, and they are counted in the total number of ordained clergy. Thus we need to consider the broad spectrum of positions in which clergy are employed to assess demand and supply. From data summarized in the Appendix (Tables 4 and 5), several generalizations can be made.[3]

First, as already noted, all denominations have experienced increases in the total number of clergy, regardless of the type of position; however, the proportion of clergy serving as parish pastors has declined relative to nonparish positions. The parish is still the major employer of clergy but less so in recent years.

Second, it follows that for all denominations there were increases in the number of nonparish ministry positions during most of the time periods for which we have data. This growth not only reflects expansion of denominational administrative positions, but a variety of church-sponsored specialized ministries—institutional and military chaplains, pastoral counselors, teachers in higher education, campus ministers, and so on. Such specialization parallels trends in other occupations and reflects the increased differentiation of American society.

Third, in several denominations—notably The Episcopal Church, the United Church of Christ, The United Methodist Church, and the United Presbyterian Church in the U.S.A.—there began to be cutbacks in these nonparish positions during the 1970s. Expansion in the 1960s was followed by contraction. A particularly striking example of a cutback (which actually began in the 1950s) occurred in The United Methodist Church's overseas mission program. In 1950 there were approximately 1,500 ordained missionaries. In 1960 there were 1,200. The number declined to 600 by 1970, and currently it is estimated at 200 to 250 persons. That represents an 83 percent decline; it is a loss of positions for ordained clergy approximately equivalent to those in two annual conferences.

Finally, there have been increases in the number of clergy in secular occupations or defined as "undesignated" by their denominations. This group includes those clergy who, by circumstance or choice, are not functioning in a church-related ministry position but still retain their credentials as clergy. For some denominations the increase has been well over 100 percent. While the growth in this category obviously reflects the choices of many clergy not to function in ecclesiastically recognized positions, it also reflects an oversupply of clergy relative to the demand.

A PARADOX: INCREASE IN CLERGY AND IN VACANT CHURCHES

While the number of clergy has increased, especially those listed as undesignated or in secular occupations, some denominations have experienced an increase in the number of parishes without clergy. The Episcopal Church, which has one of the largest increases in undesignated clergy, provides a striking illustration. At the end of 1974 there were 583 Episcopal churches vacant (without a clergyperson). This represented one out of every thirteen Episcopal congregations. Further, it was an increase of 263 vacancies as compared with the number in 1971.

Of the vacant Episcopal congregations, 77 percent had under 200 members, and many were in small towns or in rural areas. Most shared one additional significant characteristic: a budget too small to sustain a full-time priest. Both location—especially small town and rural areas some distance from large urban centers—and inadequate budgets made it difficult for such churches to attract or support full-time clergy leadership. Other denominations also have a large number of churches with fewer than 200 members, the number we suggested as typically necessary to support a full-time clergyperson. The number of churches with under 200 members is 50 percent or greater in most major Protestant denominations. Thus the potential for churches unable to support full-time clergy is quite high.

That such churches are often able to attract pastoral leadership in spite of their size or location is due to several factors. In many cases two or more congregations join in one of several possible cooperative or yoked arrangements that allow them to share the cost of a full-time pastor. Others receive denominational subsidies to bring their pastoral salaries to an agreed-upon minimum. However, inflation and other factors are increasing pressures in the denominations to discontinue such support. Still other small churches have turned to seminary students, or to other part-time or "tentmaking" styles of ministry to secure pastoral leadership. In the latter case, clergy support themselves full or part time in other occupations and provide varying amounts of pastoral leadership in the churches.

The tentmaking, or bivocational, pattern has been on the rise in several denominations, and it represents one important response to the oversupply of clergy or the corresponding decrease in demand for full-time clergy. As the number of ordained clergy increases and the number of churches able to support full-time clergy leadership decreases, the opportunity for tentmaker clergy increases. We consider tentmaking ministry more fully in chapter 9.

40

SEMINARY ENROLLMENT TRENDS

Before turning to some denominational variations in the clergy job market, we take note of enrollment trends for seminary students. Such trends are difficult to summarize succinctly; however, several observations can be made.

First, there has been a long-term increase in seminary enrollments. From 1956, the first year the Association of Theological Schools (ATS) published annual enrollment statistics, to 1977, enrollment increased by 53 percent in those schools reporting at both points in time. While there were downturns in several years, the overall trend was for increase. To be sure, not all the increase was in degree programs leading to ordination, but such programs (B.D. and M.Div.) accounted for a sizable increase.[4]

Since 1969, the year ATS began reporting the numbers by type of degree program, the number of B.D. and M.Div. *graduates* (as distinct from enrollment figures) also increased. While some seminaries have had decreases in the number of graduates since 1969 (see Appendix, Table 6), the overall number of M.Div. and B.D. graduates was 29 percent higher in 1978 than in 1969.

Another development of significance in recent years for the clergy job market is the increased number of women enrolled in seminaries, especially in programs leading to ordination. In 1972, 1,077 women students were enrolled in these programs. Six years later, in 1978, the number was 3,981, an increase of 270 percent. It is not the case, however, that this dramatic increase in women seminarians accounts for all the increase in seminary enrollments in recent years. The enrollment of men in preordination programs between 1972 and 1978 increased by 5,590, or 25 percent.

Women B.D. and M.Div. students range from a low of 4 percent of the student body in Southern Baptist Seminaries to 35 percent in UCC schools (see Appendix, Table 7). In some seminaries, such as those making up the Boston Theological Institute, women constitute approximately 50 percent of total enrollment.

Finally, we note that total seminary enrollment for black students increased from 808 students in 1970 to 1,919 in 1978, a 138 percent increase. In three- and four-year professional degree programs the number of black students increased by 99 percent from 1972 to

1978. The number of black women students has increased more rapidly than black men students. Our interview data suggests continuing serious undersupply of black ministerial candidates, in spite of the increase in seminary enrollment of blacks.

In summary, the number of persons receiving preordination degrees has increased significantly in the period from 1969 to 1978. This means that more graduates will be competing for approximately the same or even a fewer number of positions.

DENOMINATIONAL VARIATIONS IN THE CLERGY JOB MARKET

Not all denominations are similar in the relation between their supply of clergy and the demand. Based on the statistical data and on the impressions and experiences of those we interviewed, we can summarize the general situation in the late 1970s and early 1980s for the denominations we have studied. The denominations fall into three categories: those facing a current oversupply (or a decreased demand), those whose job situation is in balance but "tight," and those experiencing few or no problems.

Among denominations whose clergy are experiencing difficulty in the job market are The Episcopal Church, the Presbyterian Church in the U.S., The United Presbyterian Church in the U.S.A., the Reformed Church in America, and the United Church of Christ. All these denominations, except United Church of Christ, fall into the restricted open method of deployment; that is, they restrict a congregation's choice to those clergy who have met denomination-ally required standards. A UCC congregation is formally free to call any minister it wishes, although the typical pattern is to remain within the denomination when calling a pastor. With very few exceptions the national and regional officials of each of these denominations report a difficult job market for clergy seeking placement. There are regional variations. The Plains states, for example, which have large numbers of rather isolated small parishes, have less of an oversupply than other regions. Even there the supply has increased, with the largest gain near major urban centers.

Most of the officials interviewed from these denominations also reported a decrease in the average number of vacancies in their

42

region at any given time. A decline from an average of eight to ten, to four or five vacancies in the past five years was reported by several officials. Even when the vacancy rate has not declined significantly, the vacancies are more likely to be what one UCC conference minister described as "lean"; that is, financially marginal and relatively unattractive churches.

With the exception of The Episcopal Church most of these denominations are not having serious difficulty placing new entrants. Although their choices are more limited, most new entrants are able to find first jobs either on the staffs of large churches or as pastors of small churches. Some Episcopal bishops, however, are refusing to ordain candidates, or, contrary to church law, they are ordaining candidates without assuring them of positions within the diocese. In at least one diocese, candidates for ordination are being required to have an occupational skill in addition to their clergy training. This makes it easier for them to function as tentmakers or to support themselves in the event they are unable to secure calls.

In addition to these denominations, the other denomination experiencing some difficulties in supply and demand is The United Methodist Church. Technically, United Methodists cannot have a surplus of clergy. Each ministerial member of an annual conference is guaranteed an appointment. Nonetheless, some conferences are experiencing considerable difficulties. Others report no problems in making all their appointments and a few report continuing shortages.

Two factors in particular lead to variation in supply and demand among United Methodist annual conferences. First, United Methodist polity makes interconference mobility among clergy relatively difficult. One conference may experience an oversupplied job situation and another a shortage, but there are serious obstacles to working out a mutual solution. Second, some United Methodist conferences have appointed Local Pastors to vacant churches. These are laypersons who serve full time or part time and are authorized to preach and perform sacramental functions on a limited basis. In periods of clergy shortages, conferences have used Local Pastors to balance the appointment system. Often they have been assigned to churches that are unable to support full-time pastors. In an oversupplied situation they may be replaced by fully ordained clergy whose salaries are supplemented by the annual conferences. Such

43

use of Local Pastors as "safety valves" makes for differences in the supply and demand situation in the various conferences, a practice that may work to the detriment of Local Pastors.

Another factor that causes some placement concerns for United Methodism is the large number of persons in special appointments—ordained clergy in other than parish appointments. Many such persons are not functioning in Methodist-related organizations and are only nominally appointed to these positions by their bishops. Such persons, by virtue of their conference membership, have the right to request pastoral appointments by their bishops. Should they do so in large numbers, the system of guaranteed appointments would not survive. This is unlikely to happen, but it is perceived as a threat that other denominations do not face. In recent years a number of steps have been taken to exercise greater control over special appointments, and there are discussions of changing the ministerial status of such persons so as to remove their guarantee of pastoral appointments.

There is a second group of denominations that appears to have a balance in supply and demand at the present time; however, each reports an increasing "tightness" in the job market and limited mobility among clergy. These include Lutheran Church in America, Disciples of Christ, and American Baptist Churches in the U.S.A.

For the Lutherans a 1974 projection by the denomination's Division of Professional Leadership was of a probable clergy surplus. This has not yet materialized, due to an apparent increase in the number of clergy retiring at age sixty-five, several years earlier than in the past. Seminarians are generally able to find placement, even though they may have to transfer to synods other than their own. Synods experiencing tightness in the job market are in the Middle Atlantic states, the Midwest—both traditional areas of Lutheran strength—and in the Far West. LCA officials also report a lack of mobility throughout most parts of the system. At the same time, there is an increased restlessness among clergy who feel the need to move and cannot do so.

Among the Disciples of Christ there also appears to be a relatively balanced situation; although, again, there are regional variations. For example, in southern California there is a very tight job market, where vacancies in recent years have decreased from an average of

44

ten to fifteen per year to five or six. In several regions clergy in middle salary ranges are finding mobility limited. At the same time, however, when there are large numbers of small churches in relatively isolated communities, as in Nebraska, for example, there is a shortage of clergy. Regional Ministers (denominational area officials) seem to be considerably anxious over the placement possibilities for the large number of women clergy entering the system.

The placement of women clergy is also of great concern to American Baptist officials. Approximately 50 percent of the students in American Baptist seminaries are women. A report of a study comparing the first placement of men and women seminary graduates noted that both men and women were finding placements; however, the placement of women takes longer, tends to be at lower salaries than for men, and is more likely to be as assistant pastors or in nonlocal church settings.[5] In general, however, American Baptists, like Lutherans and Disciples, report their supply and demand situation as balanced but tight.

In addition to the concern for the placement of women, the other concern most frequently voiced by Baptist officials was the growing number of churches no longer able to support full-time clergypersons. There is an expectation that the number of bivocational clergy will increase among American Baptists.

Denominations reporting little or no problems of oversupply are the more evangelically oriented bodies. However, the less rigorous standards for ordination or licensing in some of these denominations make it even more difficult to estimate supply and demand than in the other denominations.

Southern Baptists, the largest of all Protestant groups, are a somewhat mixed case among evangelicals. There are some reports of tightness and even an oversupply of senior pastors of congregations (as opposed to ordained persons on church staffs), especially in those churches that have come to expect seminary-trained pastoral leadership.[6]

That there is some concern over the job situation for clergy is also signaled in the recent creation of a new position in a number of state conventions within the Southern Baptist Convention. The position is that of director of church-staff relations, and its function is twofold:

assisting congregations in their search for clergy, and assisting and supporting clergy who are in trouble or are seeking calls to churches. This function represents a departure from the radical congregationalism of Baptists that has traditionally insisted on complete local autonomy in matters of calling pastors.

The tightness in the job situation for Southern Baptists is also more pronounced in those traditional areas of Southern Baptist strength, such as the South and the Southwest. However, there is aggressive expansion by the denomination in other areas of the country, resulting in a need for additional clergy in these sections.

In positions other than senior pastors of congregations—such as assistant pastors, ministers of music, ministers of education, and youth ministers, all of which are ordained—the Southern Baptists report a shortage. A 1975 projection of ministerial needs in church and associational (judicatory) staff positions estimated a need for 12,000 additional full-time and 5,200 part-time staff persons by 1979. Caution was given that the survey projections probably overestimated the actual need by 20 to 40 percent.[7] In recent years there have been dramatic increases in Southern Baptist seminarians and in college students preparing for church vocations. Among the latter there was an increase of over 4,000 students, a 60 percent gain from 1970 to 1975. Whether the increased need for staff and the expansion into new areas can absorb these new ministers is a cause for concern among some Southern Baptist officials.

The other two evangelical bodies that we surveyed, the Church of God and the Church of the Nazarene, apparently do not have significant shortages of clergy, but neither do they have an oversupply. The Church of God is currently able to place all clergy without undue problems. The higher per capita giving in the denomination and the somewhat lower salary level for clergy make it possible for a considerable number of small congregations to support full-time pastors. In 1965 the Church of the Nazarene had forecast a serious shortage by 1975, but there has been an upturn in the number of clergy and a slowdown of new church development. The large increase in unassigned clergy who, according to Nazarene officials, are there by their own volition, also suggests no great shortage of clergy.

Additional evidence of the situation in evangelical bodies comes from a brief survey conducted in 1976 by the North American Baptist Conference.[8] Of the twelve denominations surveyed, only five reported shortages, and only one said that the shortage was significant. Three qualified their statements by indicating that it is a lack of "qualified pastors." The qualification suggests that the shortage may not be overly acute, and that there is an increased concern for more rigorous standards for ministers in these denominations.

A NOTE ON MINORITY ETHNIC CLERGY

In general, the demand for trained minority ethnic leadership, whether black, native American (American Indian), or Hispanic, is greater than the supply. A 1976 survey of seven Protestant denominations showed 499 native American churches being served by only sixty-eight pastors of native American origins. And the average age of these pastors (fifty-three) was much higher than that of the native American population (twenty-three).[9]

Among blacks, the largest Protestant minority ethnic group, there are generally similar shortages of trained clergy; however, the situation is considerably more complex. Most of the all-black denominations (for example, African Methodist Episcopal Church, African Methodist Episcopal Zion Church, Christian Methodist Episcopal Church, and the National and Progressive Baptist bodies) emphasize an educated ministry but have no rigid standards. One black church leader estimated that only 10 percent of the clergy in these all-black groups are seminary trained. The percentage would be considerably less in the many independent black churches that are served by bivocational pastors. What is happening in these denominations, and in some of the independent black congregations, is what some call the "push-up" effect. As black congregational members become upwardly more mobile, with increasing opportunity, they "push-up" their expectations for clergy. "They want nothing to do with an uneducated clergy," a black church leader commented. This situation has created a considerable shortage of seminary-trained black clergy in these denominations, and despite the increase in black seminarians, the supply is unlikely to meet the demand in the near future.

47

There is a similar shortage of black seminarians in the predominantly white denominations that have a significant number of black members and churches. At the same time, however, black clergy already in these denominations are experiencing some degree of "under demand" for reasons different from those experienced by white clergy. Persisting racism severely limits the mobility of black pastors, whether seminary trained or not. They are typically not called or appointed to all-white congregations except in token cases. Thus the degree to which they can move within the denomination is restricted, especially since many black churches in these denominations are small and financially marginal in their capacity to support full-time pastors.

In summary, the demand for seminary-trained black and other ethnic minority clergy considerably outstrips the supply. This is a quite different job market situation from that facing most white clergy.

Chapter 3

Why So Many Ordained Ministers?

I have already spent two years in seminary at considerable cost preparing for the ministry. If the conference refuses to admit me, this could all be wasted effort. Besides, I still feel the Lord has called me into the ministry. . . . What is happening in the church?
—Seminary student

An oversupply of clergy exists in several major Protestant denominations and a situation of balance—often tending toward oversupply—can be found in several others. To examine the causes of the situation is the purpose of this chapter.

In our analysis of the various factors affecting the supply and demand for clergy, we have found it helpful to consider the church occupational system from an open systems perspective. This gives attention to the interrelated and interdependent internal parts of the occupational system, including congregations and other employers of clergy, theological seminaries, denominational deployment offices, and the clergy themselves. Each part, while interrelated, has varying degrees of autonomy to act independently of the others. The theology of ministry and denominational polity also play important roles in the functioning of the system. How these various internal components of the system function affects the supply and demand for clergy. Additionally, an *open* systems approach calls attention to the influence of factors in the environment or context of the system. Several important influences on clergy supply and demand are environmental or contextual, factors over which the churches have little or no control.

Although the open systems approach provides a helpful way of thinking about the internal and external factors affecting supply and demand, it does not allow simple answers. It requires consideration of the interaction of multiple factors. We look first at some of the more important factors that affect the supply and demand for clergy, and then indicate how they have interacted to bring about the current situation.

FACTORS AFFECTING SUPPLY

In considering the factors that influence the supply of clergy, we begin with those factors external to the church system and then turn to those more internal.

Demographic Factors

Demographic, or population, changes brought about by dramatic changes in the birthrate during the past thirty plus years are having profound effects on a variety of institutions in American society, including the church and the supply of clergy. This can be seen in the enrollment of the theological seminaries, especially since the mid-1960s. In 1970 there were 54 percent more persons twenty to twenty-four years of age in the U.S. population than in 1960. The growth rate of this age-group from 1970 through 1980 is anticipated to be 22 percent, a slower but still sizable increase. The twenty-five to twenty-nine age-group also increased rapidly (25 percent) during the 1960s, and it was expected to increase by another 38 percent by the end of the 1970s. These two age-groups include most of those persons typically enrolled in seminary preordination degree programs, with the tendency in recent years for the average age to move upward to the mid to high twenties. No doubt some of the increase in seminary enrollment since roughly the mid-1960s can be explained by the growth of these age-groups. There was simply a greater number of persons available in the population in the typical age categories of seminarians. We might add that the projection for the twenty to twenty-four age-group in the 1980s is for a decline (14 percent); however, the twenty-five to twenty-nine age-group will grow by 6 percent and will be at its all-time high in the latter half of the decade.[1]

Demographic changes are helpful in understanding the number of people available to enter the ministry and other occupations, but they tell us nothing about the critical factor of choice. They do not explain why, for example, the number entering the ministry increased sharply during the late 1940s through most of the 1950s, while the age-groups typically enrolled in seminary and entering the ministry did not increase during this period. Demographic changes also do not explain why there have been increases in candidates for the ministry, while teaching, also suffering from severe oversupply, has experienced sharp declines in the number of persons preparing to enter elementary and secondary education, and to a lesser degree college teaching.[2] Factors other than demography were also at work.

Oversupply in Other Occupations

College enrollments soared throughout the 1950s and 1960s, partly due to demographic factors, but also because of an increased valuing of education as essential for social and economic advancement. College graduates flooded the job market in managerial and professional occupations to the point that there has been a downturn in available jobs in many occupations and professions. Medicine, always difficult to enter, has become extremely competitive. Law also is oversupplied, as are teaching and research. Graduates of business schools have been less affected by the tight job market. A study conducted late in the seventies predicted that the job market would remain tight throughout that decade and experience moderate improvements during the 1980s, but not return to the boom conditions of the 1960s.[3]

While ministry shares in the depressed labor market, the oversupply in other occupations leads some people to enter the ministry who may not have done so otherwise. These are marginal decision-makers who have considered the ministry along with other options. As other options are closed off because of the job market, the decision to try the ministry becomes more viable. How many such persons there are we do not know, but our interviews with seminary personnel suggest that the number has increased in recent years.

Additionally, the reduced demand for both college and seminary teachers has probably increased the number of seminary graduates entering parish ministry positions. Although a survey of theological students, conducted in connection with our research, showed a sizable number interested in entering college or seminary teaching later in their careers, few will have the opportunity to do so.[4]

The Changed Status of Women

A third contributor to the increase in seminarians and to the supply of clergy has been the changing role of women. Several factors have contributed to these changes. One has been the existence of a strong and vocal feminist movement that has worked for changes in denominational polity and practices that discriminate against women. Another has been the changing perceptions of what constitute appropriate occupations for women to enter. Not only ministry, but law, medicine, and even engineering have had increased women entrants. A third factor has been the considerable rise in the number of women enrolling in colleges, thus increasing the pool of persons available to enter the ministry. In 1950, women constituted less than 30 percent of the recipients of the B.A. degrees. By 1960 the proportion rose to 35 percent, and by 1972 they were 45 percent of the graduates.[5] Finally, there is the effect of the sharp decline in the birthrate since the early 1960s, especially among college-educated women. This has given women freedom to explore career options that childrearing responsibilities previously precluded. These reasons account more for the increased number of women available to enter the ministry; they do not explain why women choose to do so.

Income and Career Choice

From the perspective of labor economics, income is a major determinant of career choice and of changes in the supply of entrants into an occupation. When considering a career, individuals evaluate the economic worth of an occupation, including prospective salary and cost of training. Given the low salaries of clergy, especially relative to other professions, it may seem highly unlikely that salary improvements in recent years have played much of a part in the current oversupply of clergy.

Clergy salaries have increased in recent years (see Appendix, Figure 1). While precise comparable data is difficult to secure due to the different denominational reporting systems, the figures indicate that the median clergy income (cash salary, value of housing, utilities, and fees) increased from $5,472 in 1956 to $10,583 in 1973, a gain of 93 percent. From 1968 to 1973, the period when the oversupply apparently began to develop in several denominations, the increase in salaries was 30 percent. Thus, insofar as salary is of concern to persons choosing the ministry as a career, some of the increase in entry is conceivably reflected in improvements over the years.

The gains, however, are more apparent than real. When the buying power of the dollar is held constant, it is discovered that the greatest improvement came during the late 1950s and early 1960s. From 1968 to 1973, the improvement was only 2 percent in constant dollars. Insofar as individuals consider the buying power of clergy income, the increases are not likely to account for the growth in seminary enrollments since the mid to late 1960s. We are led therefore to give little weight to salary as a prominent factor in the oversupply. When compared with salaries in other occupations, it is rather remarkable that there is an oversupply or increase in seminary enrollment. A recent magazine article comparing the worst and best careers for the 1980s drew the following blunt conclusions: "From a secular point of view, a career in the Protestant churches promises little. Ministers are in vast oversupply and the pay is terrible."[6] Individuals do not enter the ministry with salary considerations as a primary motivation.

The Religious Climate and Career Choice

Quite a number of persons interviewed attributed the increased number preparing for ordained ministry to the current religious climate. Both among older adults and college-aged youth there seems to be a renewal of religious concern. Much, though not all, has roots in both the evangelical and charismatic movements and tends to have a conservative cast. The large increases since 1970 of students in Southern Baptist colleges preparing for church careers is a fruit of this renewal.

In one sense this is cause for rejoicing. Despite the already crowded job market for clergy, the increase in candidates may be God's way of calling the church to a new awakening. This is the interpretation that a number of evangelical church leaders and seminarians place on the situation. In fact, some make the interesting suggestion that previous evangelical awakenings were preceded by an increased number of clergy. To our knowledge, no historian has attempted to demonstrate this linkage.

The Impact of Past Supply and Demand Dynamics

Thus far, the factors considered have focused primarily on the choice of ministry as a career. Nevertheless, over- or undersupply is also influenced by the number of ministers already in the church system. When we consider that the length of a typical minister's career is approximately thirty to forty years, we recognize how decreased or increased numbers of clergy entering the system at one point in time can have long-term consequences.

During the depression years of the 1930s there was a serious oversupply of clergy in many Protestant denominations. An important cause was the economic situation; many churches could no longer afford clergy. A 1934 article described the situation:

> The burden of the depression has fallen most heavily upon ministers of the Protestant groups. The diversity and variety of these groups make this inevitable. The ministers of the denominations most highly centralized (Episcopal and Methodist) have suffered the least. . . . The ministers of the more loosely organized denominations such as the Disciples of Christ, the Baptists, the Congregationalists, and the Presbyterians have suffered the most unemployment. The figures have not been compiled, but it seems quite clear that no fewer than 30,000 ministers of the Protestant faith are without employment. Of this number, it would be safe to say that fully one-third would normally be without posts.[7]

The reaction to the oversupply was not unlike that today. Presbyterians called for a tightening of entrance requirements in seminaries: "The church has now more available ministers than it can employ and therefore the time is opportune for rigidly enforcing regulations that will heighten the intellectual standard and corresponding efficiency of our ministers."[8] The Ohio Conference of the Methodist Episcopal Church refused to admit for one year any new ministers on trial.[9]

From the available data it appears that there was some decline in the number of ordinations during the 1930s, possibly in response to

54

the oversupply. The total number of ministers declined during this period in all denominations for which we have data. Evidently, many of those who could not find church positions took jobs outside the church. By the late 1930s there were worries over declining seminary enrollments and a prediction of an acute shortage of clergy in the near future.[10]

World War II affected the supply of clergy during the 1940s. Ordinations increased in the first few years of the decade, then fell again through the remaining years. All the denominations for which we have data experienced slight increases in the annual number of ordinations in the 1940s as compared with the 1930s, ranging from 1 percent in The Episcopal Church to 14 percent in the Congregational Christian Churches. The total number of clergy remained relatively stable.

At war's end there was the beginning of the religious revival that lasted through the next decade. These were boom years for the churches; membership grew and new congregations were organized. Concerns were expressed about the shortage of clergy, and considerable energy was expended to recruit new ministers. The effort bore fruit; ordinations increased sharply in all denominations.

The persons who entered the ordained ministry during the 1930s are now reaching retirement. Thus there are few clergy eligible to retire at a time when large numbers of persons are available to enter the ministry. However, the number of persons reaching retirement (assuming that age 65 will continue to be the norm) will increase sharply during the late 1980s and early 1990s, as those who entered in the postdepression years become eligible to retire. An illustration of the effects of past supply and demand relationships is shown in the Appendix (Figure 2). It presents the age distribution of Presbyterian Church in the United States clergy in five-year intervals at seven points in time (the last three are projections based on current data). In the 1958 graph, the effects of smaller numbers of clergy entering in the 1930s and 1940s (and apparently earlier as well) are evident. There are relatively small numbers of older clergy. Also obvious is the influence of the sharp increase in entrants in the 1950s. Moving across the twenty-year period, an increasingly older group of clergy is evident. But also, through 1975, there is a decreasing number who are sixty-five or older; that is, who are of retirement age. The sixty to sixty-four category (candidates for retirement) was quite low, relative to the younger categories, and remained so through 1968, when it began to rise. With the sharply increased number of entrants in the 1950s, which slowed only modestly through the 1960s, and the relatively low number of persons of retirement age through the early 1970s, it is easy to see how an oversupply might have developed if demand did not keep pace with supply. As can be seen, the 1978 and 1983 graphs show an increase in the number reaching retirement age.

In other denominations the pattern of increasing retirements also seems likely. In The Episcopal Church 155 clergy reached age 65 in 1977. The number will increase to 180 by 1982, to 204 in 1987, and to 334 in 1992. The latter year is when a person who entered the ministry at age 25 in 1952 can retire. The Lutheran Church in America had 91 clergy to reach age 65 in 1977; by 1982 there will be 132. There will be 147 in 1987 and 200 in 1992. In the Church of God (Anderson, Indiana) 78 ministers reached age 65 in 1977. Unlike the other denominations, the number will remain relatively constant; it will increase to 94 in 1987 and drop to 86 in 1992.

Available United Methodist age data was grouped differently from the others. In that denomination 2,522 clergy reached retirement age between 1974 and 1978. Between 1979 and 1983 the number will grow to 3,162; and between 1989 and 1993, it will increase to 3,868. While the Methodist pattern is generally similar to the other denominations, the proportional increase in retirements in the future is not as large.

These projected retirement figures make no allowance for mortality of clergy prior to age sixty-five or for early retirements and withdrawals. They suggest, nevertheless, that there may be the beginning of an easing of the oversupply through retirements, and that the likelihood of this will increase as we move into the mid to late 1980s. By the early 1990s there could be a shortage of clergy if there should be a drop in the number of entrants.

Past supply and demand dynamics are important influences on the present situation. Likewise, the supply and demand relationships of the recent past and present will make their effect felt in future years. It is important to keep the long-range picture in view as strategies are considered to relieve the present imbalance.

FACTORS AFFECTING DEMAND

In this section some of the factors that determine the demand for clergy and changes that have influenced the current situation are considered. Demand for clergy is determined by several factors that may be stated as questions:

1. What are the services for which ordained clergy, as distinct from laity, are needed to perform?
2. How elastic or flexible is the need for these services?
3. What is the cost of these services relative to other costs?

These are exceedingly complex questions that we will not attempt to answer directly. Rather, they will be considered somewhat indirectly, as we examine several factors that have brought about changes in the demand for clergy in recent years.

Church Membership Growth and Decline

The number of church members has an obvious impact on the demand for clergy. An increase in membership occurs as existing congregations grow larger or as new congregations are established. In either case there is an increased demand for clergy as principal pastors or as additional staff.

It is difficult to generalize about how many ordained clergy are needed per lay member. The answer depends on the services for which ordained clergy are deemed necessary to perform, as well as on the size of the congregation. Some maintain that 500 members is the upper limit for whom a single pastor can effectively assume responsibility. Others put the figure at 350. Much, however, depends on the degree to which laity share the ministry of the church. In high-sharing churches less professional leadership may be required. Nonetheless, change in membership size is an important influence on the demand for clergy.

There was considerable church membership growth in the 1950s and early 1960s. Although part of that growth was in existing congregations, much was in new church development. The National Council of Churches reported that 3,198 new local churches were established between 1954 and 1957.[11] However, membership trends since the mid-1960s have been quite different for many denominations—notably those that are also experiencing an oversupply. They have lost members, while the more evangelical churches, who are typically not experiencing a clergy oversupply, have continued to grow.

New church development also reflects these trends. The number of new congregations decreased sharply in the more liberal denominations but considerably less so in the evangelical churches. From 1960 to 1966 United Church of Christ new congregations declined by 65 percent. The United Presbyterians, who had averaged seventy churches per year from 1950 through 1962, averaged only thirty per year between 1963 and 1973. Southern Baptist new church development also declined by 36 percent from 1963 to 1973, with an overall average of ninety-five new churches per year.

Obviously, such changes in membership, whether in existing congregations or in new churches, have influenced the demand for clergy. The effect since the mid-1960s, with the exception of the evangelical churches, has been to reduce the demand.

Changes in the Number of Nonparish Positions
Related to membership trends have been both growth and decline in the number of nonparish ministry positions. Membership growth and decline influence the demand for support services for parishes. During the 1950s and 1960s there was an increase in nonparish positions, many of which were created to respond to local church needs. This included regional judicatory staff, as well as staff in the various national boards and agencies that provide program resources and other services for congregations.

Additionally, church bureaucracies engage in activities at regional, national, and international levels that local churches are not equipped to do, such as mission efforts both in this country and abroad. These agencies too have grown over the years, and many of the new positions they have created have been filled by clergy.

Also, as is well known, there is a variety of other nonparish positions that employ clergy, some of which are under church auspices and others with secular sponsorship. They include teachers in educational institutions, chaplaincies, campus ministries, staff in a variety of ecumenical agencies, and especially during the 1960s, staff in various social services and social action programs, often under government sponsorship.

58

Thus, to meet a variety of needs, there has been a growing number of positions in nonparish settings which it has seemed appropriate and/or necessary for ordained clergy to fill. While we may question the necessity of ordination for many of these positions, it is nevertheless the case that many clergy have found employment in them.

The demand in these areas grew considerably during the high-growth years of the church, in the 1950s and early to mid-1960s. Since the late 1960s and early 1970s, however, there have been declines in the number of such positions. The decreases have been for a variety of reasons: demographic changes, which have been a factor in both church membership declines and in decreasing college enrollment; shifts in denominational priorities; changes in the understanding of the missionary task of the church; restructuring of denominational bureaucracies; declining church membership; and probably most important of all, declining revenues and rising costs. One denominational executive who was interviewed speculated that cutbacks of positions would have been even greater in some national denominational agencies had spending not been reduced to maintain personnel.

Consequently, demand for clergy was first raised by the growth in these nonparish positions and then lowered as the positions have been cut back. To use economic terminology, the demand for these positions and for the services they provide is more elastic (or flexible) than that of parish ministry positions. If services have to be cut back, it is less likely that they will be those provided by parish clergy and much more likely to be those in the nonparish areas.

Congregational Viability and Demand for Clergy

Demand for clergy is also affected by the amount of clergy leadership congregations can afford. Most judicatory executives with whom we talked used either membership size or the size of the church's budget as rules of thumb, but all confessed lack of a precise answer. Budget size implies the ability to afford full-time clergy leadership or additional staff. Congregational size has a relation to the size of the budget (more precisely to giving), and it also determines, in part, whether a given parish provides an adequate work load for a full-time pastor and additional staff.

The trends in the ratio of church members to clergy and in clergy to churches, as we saw in Table 1, have been for ministers, on the average, to serve increasingly fewer church members and for there to be fewer clergy per church. The norm implicit in these trends is that of a minimum of one full-time pastor per congregation, and many congregations have bought into that norm. Attempts to achieve the norm have been made through subdividing circuits or yoked churches. In many instances denominations have provided salary subsidies to make this possible. This trend and that of creating new staff positions in larger congregations have prevented the present oversupply of clergy from being even more serious.

Data from a 1973 study of clergy support was used to construct an index of the membership and budget size needed to enable a congregation to employ a pastor full time (see Appendix, Table 8). We found considerable variations by denomination. A Church of God congregation can support a full-time pastor with a much smaller membership than all other denominations. United Methodists fall on the other end of the spectrum, requiring the largest number of members to support full-time pastoral leadership. With the exception of these two denominations, a good rule of thumb is 200 members needed to support a full-time minister. When we recall that in most denominations at least 50 percent of the congregations have fewer than 200 members, it becomes clear that the implicit norm of one clergy per church can at best be only half accomplished.

We have no trend data that might show changes in the necessary minimum size for full-time leadership, but we expect it has increased in recent years under the pressure of inflation. The increased number of vacant Episcopal parishes seems to bear this out; many small congregations can no longer afford to employ a pastor full time.

As for the other trend, that of adding full-time staff in larger congregations, we have no index other than the previously noted rule of thumb that a full-time clergyperson is needed for every 500 members. If changes in church size are indicative, the trend toward adding staff has slowed or reversed, thus reducing demand. Reflecting membership trends, most of the mainline denominations have experienced declining numbers of larger congregations. Southern Baptists provide a contrast; between 1964 and 1974 they experienced gains of 20 percent or more in all church size categories except for those under 300 members.

In summary, increasing the demand for clergy by providing full-time ministerial leadership for small congregations, or by adding staff in larger congregations, has probably reached its upper limit in many denominations. The pressures of inflation and membership losses have combined to slow, if not reverse, the trend.

PUTTING IT ALL TOGETHER

The supply of clergy has two components: the supply of new entrants into the ministry and the supply already in the system. The post-World War II years, down through the early 1960s, were growth years for the churches, including growth in new entrants into the ministry. Although there were modest declines in new entrants in the late 1960s and early 1970s, the demographic situation, the feminist movement, the overall job market, and the present religious ferment have combined to increase the number of current seminarians and entering clergy.

At the same time, the impact of past supply and demand imbalance has been felt in the flow through the church system of the existing supply of clergy. Low entry into the ministry in past years has created a situation of fewer retirements at a time when there are a large number of entrants.

From the side of demand for clergy, membership growth (including new church development), the rapid expansion of nonparish ministry positions, and the increasing number of churches desiring full-time, ordained leadership or additional staff, greatly increased the demand for clergy throughout the post-World War II years and into the mid-1960s. This resulted in a psychology of clergy shortage.

Beginning about 1965 demand began to be affected as church membership declines set in and new church development slowed. By the early 1970s economic and other pressures brought cutbacks in nonparish ministry positions, which reduced demand and also increased the supply of active clergy seeking available positions. Finally, rising costs of goods and services, and losses of membership combined to slow, if not reverse, the trend toward full-time clergy for small congregations and additional staff for large congregations. The result is the current oversupply of clergy or at least an increasingly tight job market.

We emphasize that this has occurred in some but not all denominations. In several of the more evangelical denominations the demand has generally kept pace with the supply. They have continued to grow in membership and to start new churches. They have been pinched by inflation, as have all churches, but some have both high per capita giving and relatively low salary requirements for clergy that have worked to keep demand high.

AND THE FUTURE?

It is a hazardous business to forecast the future; however, the review of the various trends and the attempt to specify the multiple factors affecting supply and demand for clergy enable us to make some informed guesses. One thing is clear. The future situation, as the past and present have been, will be influenced by multiple factors. Straight-line projections, such as those in chapter 2, are useful to show us what the trend will be, other things being equal. But other things are rarely equal, and the future is never surprise-free. Even the multiple factors we have considered are not necessarily sufficient predictions of the future. Nevertheless, several things can be said on the basis of them.

The supply of new entrants into the ministry is likely to continue to increase through the 1980s. Demographic conditions will continue to be favorable through that time, especially if the trend to somewhat older entrants continues. The tight job situation in other occupations will continue to influence some who are marginal decision-makers to consider the ministry, although reports of oversupply in the ministry could also discourage some candidates. The impact of the feminist movement is likely to continue, although it may have already reached a plateau as far as growth is concerned.

By the mid-1980s and continuing through the early 1990s the job market in other occupations may improve slightly, but it is still expected to be somewhat difficult for college-trained persons. This improvement may slightly counterbalance the effects of the demographic situation by reducing the number of marginal decision-makers entering the ministry.

There is no reason to believe that the number of women entrants will decline in the mid to late 1980s; however, neither is it likely that this number will increase significantly. Much will depend on the acceptance or rejection experienced by the large number of women currently preparing for ordination. Should they experience general acceptance and find mobility possible, there could be an increase in women entrants. Continued resistance could bring a negative reaction.

The supply of clergy already in the system will decline as a result of increased retirements by the mid to late 1980s. At least through 1985 the effects of the current oversupply are likely to continue to be felt because of the large number of clergy currently in most church systems, and because of the probable continued growth in entrants. From the mid-1980s through the mid-1990s large increases in retirements could bring about a shortage of clergy. However, since demographic conditions tend to favor a growing number of entrants, the effects of retirements could be minimal.

The factors that affect the demand for clergy are more difficult to forecast. Church membership declines of the past decade or more may have bottomed out. There are, in fact, some signs of a possible period of increase. This will come partly as a result of the attention denominations, including many of those that have been in decline, are beginning to give to church growth and new church development. Furthermore, the demographic situation through the next two decades will favor church growth, other things being equal. That is, the age-group most likely to be active church members—the thirty-five to fifty-four age-group, especially those with school-aged children—will increase in the population through the year 2000. If church growth does occur, as it is likely to do as a result of these pressures, the demand for clergy could increase.

At the same time, however, it is not clear what the situation will be for nonparish ministries or for increasing the number of full-time ministers in small congregations. Economic forecasts of continuing inflation, coupled with a possible recession, suggest that there will not likely be much increase in nonparish ministries unless they are self-supporting. For the same reason it is unlikely that small churches will increase their demand for full-time clergy. If anything, economic pressures will continue to increase the number of small churches that can no longer afford full-time clergy. If church membership increases, there may be some increase in parish ministry staff positions.

Religious awakenings are impossible to predict. If the churches experience a significant revival, and many feel this is a strong possibility, the future could be vastly different from what the present trends would indicate.

Part II

Consequences of the Clergy Oversupply

Chapter 4

Consequences for the Clergy

A judicatory official, whose responsibility includes the placement of ministers, expresses his frustration to a colleague: "I have several younger pastors who are doing a first-rate job. They are capable of serving larger churches, but I do not have any places to which I can promote any of them."

A dean of a prominent theological seminary reports to his faculty, "Five of our recent graduates were denied ordination by their regional judicatory." This rarely happens to alumni of this school. Five rejections by the same committee is without precedent. The dean looks troubled; the faculty is shocked.

The persons most affected by the current oversupply of clergy are the ministers themselves. The ways in which the tight job market is having an impact on the clergy is the subject of this chapter.

ADMISSION TO THE ORDAINED MINISTRY

The oversupply of clergy is having a significant effect on admission to the ordained ministry. In the days of a ministerial shortage, denominational officials courted seminary students, and pastors of local churches were urged to recruit youth for the ministry. Strict admission requirements have usually been the rule, but when clergy were in short supply, exceptions could be made. The rigorous standards could be relaxed, and the applicant about whom there was some question could be given a chance.

The present oversupply of clergy has resulted in a drastically changed situation. The church boards that screen applicants are now interpreting the high requirements more strictly. They know that they will have to say no to some persons and need to have reasons for doing so. Thus the seminary graduate who gives evidence of either lack of commitment to the ministry or inadequate preparation may be rejected. One judicatory board that reviews candidates annually has simply been refusing to consider individuals who do not meet the timetable for completing the various required stages in submitting such items as a theological statement, a sermon, and so forth. This has the effect of reducing the number of persons on whom the board must make a judgment by eliminating some on technicalities. At the same time, judicatories are requiring an increasing number of specific courses that candidates must have completed before admission.

The oversupply has made the admission process more hazardous for the candidate. A higher proportion are being rejected than was the case five or ten years ago. Graduation from a good theological seminary will no longer assure that the individual will be admitted into the ministry.

In a tight job market, factors other than the applicant's competency are being considered. The tendency is for regional judicatories to give preference to ministerial candidates who come from the member churches. Only if there are additional vacancies are persons from outside the judicatory considered.

FIRST POSITIONS

Seminary graduates who are accepted by their denomination are, in most cases, finding it possible to find positions either as pastors of congregations or as members of church staffs. The major reason for this is the large number of relatively small-membership churches. As previously noted, more than half the congregations in the major Protestant denominations have fewer than 200 members. These churches provide modest salaries that are acceptable to young ministers just beginning their careers.

Some denominations have a minimum salary, an amount that a congregation is required to pay a full-time pastor. The denomination may provide a subsidy to bring the pastor's salary up to the amount required. Many small congregations pay their young and inexperienced ministers the necessary minimum or slightly more.

The oversupply of clergy, however, is giving the beginning pastor fewer options. While the recent graduate can usually secure a parish, he or she may not be able to secure employment in a particular part of the country, a city of a certain size, or a desired type of community. The person who needs a specific area because of a spouse's place of employment may encounter great difficulty. Some judicatory executives are finding this to be almost as serious a hindrance to the employment of married women who are clergy as the resistance of congregations to clergywomen. The seminary graduate who is able to relocate and who does not have too many preconditions to be met can secure a church.

LIMITATIONS ON MOBILITY

The ministry tends to be an occupation characterized by mobility. While the length of time a pastor may stay in the same church varies in different denominations, a great deal of moving from congregation to congregation is the rule. Promotion, for most ministers, means moving to a different parish.

The oversupply of clergy has slowed down ministerial mobility. One denominational executive compares the present situation to an overcrowded expressway, where the sheer volume has reduced movement to a crawl. He comments. "The entrance ramps are getting so crowded that it is even difficult to get on."

Because there may be no place to which a pastor can move, or perhaps more accurately, no larger church to which he or she wants to move, the tendency is to stay put. There also appears to be a self-fulfilling prophecy at work. Clergy hear that there is an oversupply and decide not to attempt a move even when they desire or need to move. The result of these choices is a slowing down of the entire system. Ministers in denominations in which congregations call their pastors are more affected by this situation than those in denominations that assign clergy. In the latter it is possible to move a pastor, even if only laterally, to a similar church.

Certain types of clergy have handicaps that make mobility

particularly difficult in a time of oversupply. Persons over fifty-five often find it difficult to secure calls should they need to relocate. A congregation is very reluctant to call a minister in that age-range, apparently feeling they will have him or her until retirement. The older minister may be forced to accept a small church and a sharply reduced salary. The case of Jim, in chapter 1, is an example. In this case, his divorce provided an additional handicap in securing another position.

A lack of mobility also causes morale problems for some clergy and congregations. In some instances clergy find themselves growing stale in their job performance. As a presbytery executive described the situation, "Some ministers have a bag of tricks that lasts about four years. They have been accustomed to moving after that. Now that they can't move, either they must develop new skills and fresh insights or they grow stale, and their morale and effectiveness suffer." It may be that the lack of ability to move psychologically blocks creative responses in the person's present location. A United Church of Christ conference minister cited a case of a pastor who wanted to move and who came to him with an outline of plans for his next parish. "He was unable to visualize how he might implement these same plans in his present parish."

There are instances when both the clergyperson and the congregation would benefit from a move. Because he or she cannot get a call, both pastor and people continue a less-than-satisfactory relationship that is debilitating to both.

THE MIDCAREER CRISIS

The most serious impact of the oversupply of clergy comes at what may be called the midcareer crisis. This critical period has an obvious relationship to the so-called midlife transition, about which much has been written in recent years. To understand this situation, one needs to consider the way most clergy expect their careers to proceed. A clergyperson may anticipate starting in a small, possibly rural, church (or churches, often serving two or more congregations). With experience he or she moves to a somewhat larger congregation, perhaps a single church in a county seat. Each move is to a larger congregation, one which carries more responsibility, prestige, and salary.

Of course, not every minister's career proceeds in this manner. The relatively few large congregations, compared with the very large number of small- and medium-sized ones, mean that only a small proportion of clergy will reach the "high steeple" churches. Many persons have arrived at their early forties and realized that they, for any number of reasons, are not going to become president of the company or pastor of First Church. This often precipitates the midcareer crisis. This situation is aggravated by two factors at the present time. The first is the increasing tendency for clergy to measure their own and their peers' success in the ministry by both the size and prestige of the church they serve. The criteria are almost exclusively institutional measures. There is a pervasive ecclesiastical success ethic that equates bigness with achievement. United Methodist district superintendents often remind congregations that the higher the salaries they pay, the better pastors they will receive, a myth not necessarily borne out by facts. While a church offering a high salary can be assured of a large number of applicants when a vacancy occurs, the salary received is not necessarily positively correlated with either the pastor's commitment to the faith or her or his competency in ministerial skills.

The second complicating factor is the current shortage of positions, which has limited mobility for many clergy. With fewer openings there are fewer positions into which a minister might move, especially ones considered desirable. Thus an individual who would like to be promoted to a larger church may have only the opportunity to move laterally, to a similar church, or not even have the chance to move anywhere. In 1976 the United Presbyterian Vocation Agency reported that for every vacant church offering to pay a salary of $14,000 or more, there were sixteen pastors available among those seeking a change. Only 1.5 pastors wanting to relocate were available for vacant churches paying $9,000 or less.[1] In a tight job market the pastor wishing to relocate simply will have fewer options.

The midcareer crisis tends to come about the minister's third or fourth move out of seminary. Consider the case of a pastor who, upon graduation, received a call to a small church. He did well and five years later moved to another church where, from all indications, he has been having an effective ministry. Now he is thirty-seven. His children are about to enter high school, and college is not far in the future. With his experience he feels ready for the challenge and responsibility of a larger church. The small-town church he is now serving is not going to grow or change in the foreseeable future. In fact, he is both ready for and able to serve the type of church he would like to secure. The problem is that there are several other ministers for every opening. There are simply more persons qualified to receive a promotion than there are places to which they can be promoted.

The realization that one is not likely to achieve anticipated goals and that one's career has peaked, can be a devastating experience. It can affect not only the individual's performance, but his or her sense of self-worth. For some, it may result in a decision to leave the ordained ministry, or worse, to remain, but doing so with a sense of failure and defeat.

The midcareer crisis is not a new phenomenon, of course. Persons frequently experience the frustration of not achieving the desired career goals; however, the present job market has made this problem more serious as more clergy are affected and cannot move to the kinds of churches they may be equipped to serve or even move at all.

JOB SECURITY

The present oversupply of clergy may make the ministry a less secure occupation than it has been in the recent past. As church members become increasingly aware that clergy are available, there will be less reluctance to terminate a pastor with whom the congregation, for whatever reason, has become dissatisfied.

However, the impact of the current job market has not had as drastic an effect on the minister's job security as might be assumed. There are several reasons for this. The first is the tradition of the free pulpit: the concept that a pastor should be free to preach and to act as he or she feels God wills, even if the members of the congregation disagree.

Second, many clergy have a form of tenure. One example is the United Methodist pastor who, while moving frequently, has tenure within the annual conference and is assured another appointment. The Episcopal priest also has tenure in the parish as does the

Presbyterian pastor, although the latter can be removed by the presbytery.

A long-term oversupply will put serious strain on these tenure systems. With more clergy than positions, a congregation will be less willing to retain an unpopular or ineffective pastor. In spite of the tenure of an Episcopal priest, the congregation has a way of securing a rector's resignation. In fact, there is already a trend in The Episcopal Church toward term contracts instead of tenure. Also, persons who see their promotions thwarted by a tenure system will not continue to support that system. The trend will be toward congregationalism, with the local church deciding which pastor it will employ and for how long, with less control being exercised by denominational officials. At present there is movement in this direction. The United Methodists' recent requirement of consultation between the bishop, clergy, and congregation with regard to appointments is an example.

The third reason why the oversupply has not had a greater effect on the minister's job security is that many local church people do not realize that an oversupply exists. They still assume that they may have trouble replacing a pastor who resigns or is terminated. A member of a large downtown church whose rector had resigned asked, "Do you think we'll have any difficulty finding someone who wants to come here?" This situation will change as more laity become aware of the current job market.

LEAVING THE MINISTRY

It has been impossible to determine with any degree of accuracy the extent to which the oversupply is causing persons to leave the ministry. There is evidence that some persons who feel their mobility is blocked have decided to change careers. Some persons have not been able to secure pastorates and have been forced to seek other employment. However, most persons who have withdrawn from the ministry due to the tight job situation appear to have done so, not because they could not find parishes, but because they could not secure the kinds of parishes they desired.

Probably a more significant factor has been the willingness of some judicatories to deal with the person who may be in the wrong profession. There are clergy who, for a wide range of reasons, are not effective. In a time when there was a shortage of pastors, church officials were reluctant to terminate a minister whose performance tended to be substandard. With replacements difficult to secure, the individual whose ability may have been judged less than adequate was retained. In The United Methodist Church the practice has often been to move an ineffective pastor frequently, from one church to another, with little or no effort to assist the person to develop increased competence or to leave the ordained ministry with dignity.

There is evidence that judicatories are becoming more willing to deal with the incompetent minister. Denominational officials report increased counseling with such persons. Frequently, the individual is assisted in finding another type of employment. This may be done quietly and informally. In some cases, judicatories have developed exit procedures to assist pastors who are terminated or who cannot secure churches. These tend to include such factors as termination pay for a limited period of time, payment for job counseling, and assistance with the moving expenses if relocation is required. Different practices are found in the various denominations, but the goal is to treat the person leaving the ministry fairly and assist him or her to find an alternative career. We note, however, that one of the most serious obstacles to the termination of the clergy relationship comes from fellow clergy in the judicatory, who often are required to vote in matters of termination. There develops what some have called the "there-but-for-the-grace-of-God-go-I" stance. Fellow clergy resist voting to terminate one of their own, however much it may be best for the individual and the denomination.

The impact of the oversupply, as described in this chapter, applies equally to men and women who are clergy. Because of the increase in the number of clergywomen in the 1970s and the special problems they face, an entire chapter has been devoted to their situation. To this subject we now turn.

Chapter 5

Sisters in the Brotherhood

The 1970s will be remembered as the decade in which large numbers of women entered the ranks of the ordained Protestant clergy. Women ministers are not a new phenomenon. Pentecostal churches and The Salvation Army have long had substantial numbers of clergywomen; several mainline denominations have had ordained and unordained women ministers for many years. A variety of professional church leadership roles have been filled by women, including congregational staff jobs and positions in church-related institutions. Both single and married women have played a significant part in the missionary force at home and abroad. The deaconess movement has provided credentials and certain benefits—such as placement, pensions, and retirement homes—for a group of professional churchworkers.

The present decade is different from previous periods in two respects: (1) a large number of women have enrolled in and are now graduating from theological seminaries, and (2) most are seeking ordination and careers as pastors of congregations or positions appropriate for ordained persons.

THE INCREASING NUMBER OF CLERGYWOMEN

The increase in the number of clergywomen has been a significant event of the 1970s. A 1977 survey of seventy-six denominations by the National Council of Churches reported 10,470 clergywomen, or 4 percent of all the ministers in seventy-six denominations.[1] The United Presbyterian Church in the U.S.A. had 76 ordained women in 1970, and 248 in 1976, a gain of 226 percent. The Presbyterian

Church in the United States reported 98 women seminary graduates in early 1976, with 80 more women expected to graduate in the next two years.

The Episcopal Church, which until 1976 did not ordain women, anticipates that there will soon be 200 ordained women. Women make up 18 percent of the students pursuing divinity degrees in Episcopal seminaries. Between 1961 and 1968 The Methodist Church averaged 260 women under appointment, which included ordained and lay pastors assigned by bishops as pastors of congregations or to some other ministerial positions. There are now over 600 ordained women in that denomination.

The number of women enrolled in theological schools indicates that there will be a substantial increase in the number of women ministerial candidates in the period ahead. The more liberal seminaries have had the largest influx of women. While the increase of women students appears to have slowed slightly since the mid-1970s, there are no signs of a reversal of the trend.

The more conservative schools seem to be two to four years behind the more liberal schools, with regard to the proportion of women students in degree programs leading to ordination. However, while the proportion of women in preordination degree programs in the conservative seminaries is still small, it too is growing. For some time these schools have had a substantial number of women students in degree programs that do not lead to ordination, but they are now enrolling more in the M.Div. programs. They appear to be at the point where their liberal counterparts were in 1972 and 1973, and are moving in the same direction.

If the proportion of women enrolled in seminaries remains at the level of the academic years 1975 through 1978, the church will have approximately one woman graduate with the educational requirements for ordination for every nine men. If the number of women enrolled in the more conservative seminaries approaches that of the liberal schools, the proportion of women ministerial candidates could be one fourth to one third the total.

WHY NOW?

Why has the increase in women ministerial candidates occurred at this particular time? In terms of the clergy job market, there has not been a worse time for an increase in women ministerial candidates since the depression of the 1930s. Women entrants are not responding to a desperate need for pastors to fill vacant pulpits. During the shortage of pastors in the 1950s there was no increase in the number of women candidates. Neither is the growing number of women clergy the result of a religious revival among women. Rather, the sharp increase in the number of women entering and preparing for the ministry seems to be the result of the feminist movement in American society. This movement, which is attempting to eliminate social and economic differences based on sex, is having a profound effect on many institutions, and the church and the ministry are no exception. This can be noted in the style of rhetoric, the concern over perceived real and symbolic insults—such as anger toward the historian who lectures on the *fathers* of the early church—the hostility toward male colleagues and other women who deviate from the movement's norms, the emphasis given to achieving positions of prestige and high salary in the denominational organizations, and the attempt to rewrite theology from a woman's perspective. Without the feminist movement in the larger society, the situation within the churches would be vastly different.

However, it would be absurd to claim that the women's movement was solely responsible for the increase in the women clergy. The individual's motivation for entering the ministry is deeply personal, varied, and complex. Women make this decision for as many reasons as do men, including a clear and definite call from God to be ministers.

We are of the opinion that the entrance of a large number of women into the ranks of the Protestant clergy is, in the main, a very positive phenomenon. Any organization that increases the pool of potential leaders would benefit. The growing number of clergywom-en will result in changes in the church, some of which will be viewed as desirable and others as undesirable. It is not an overstatement to say that whatever the reason for the increase in the number of women clergy, Protestant denominations will never be quite the same again.

CHURCH RESPONSES

How are the churches responding to the increase in the number of women clergy and candidates for the ministry? The answer is that different denominations are responding differently, but the trend seems toward greater acceptance and employment of ordained women.

On one end of the spectrum are the denominations that do not yet ordain women or those that have only recently done so (for example, The Episcopal Church and the Reformed Church in America). It seems evident that pressure from women and their allies will bring changes in the denominations which do not yet ordain or are reluctant to employ women clergy.

At the other end of the spectrum are those denominations that not only ordain women, but are making special efforts in their behalf. Some have established and are funding agencies or units within existing agencies to work on behalf of women. The official stance of denominations such as American Baptist Churches in the U.S.A., the Lutheran Church in America, two Presbyterian bodies, the Disciples of Christ, the United Church of Christ, and The United Methodist Church is clear.

The trend among an increasing number of denominations at the national level is to affirm clergywomen and to attempt to assist them in securing appropriate positions. Church bureaucracies have been employing more women; some have established quotas to ensure a minimum number. While all churches have not moved at the same speed, the trend toward greater efforts to support the aspirations of women clergy is evident.

In most denominations it is the middle or regional judicatory that admits candidates to the ministry and assigns them to churches, or helps arrange their employment. The regional judicatories are in fact ordaining women, although some women candidates have felt they were more carefully scrutinized by examining committees than were male candidates. However, women are not being excluded; they are being ordained in increasing numbers and thus are eligible for calls from or appointments to congregations.

While experiences of women vary considerably in the degree that they have found regional judicatories to be helpful in their placement, the judicatories and other aspects of a denomination's formal deployment system play a vital role. A study of American Baptist women clergy indicated that informal channels of locating positions have not been particularly effective. (There is not yet an "old girl" network to parallel the "old boy" network.) Women have been much more successful in locating jobs through the formal placement structures. Those who pursued all channels of the formal system were successful in securing employment. For those women who totally ignored the formal system, 83 percent did not secure employment. There was no relation for clergymen between securing employment and the type of job search system used.[2]

In most Protestant denominations the congregation has a great deal of autonomy. The local group has the final decision as to who is an acceptable pastor. An affirmative action program by the denomination and the regional judicatory is, in final analysis, dependent on the action of members of the local church, and it is at the congregational level that the resistance to clergywomen has been the strongest. Nevertheless, women are being employed by congregations in increasing numbers.

Protestant churches have typically had male clergy, while a majority of their members and leaders have been women (although men have tended to be the majority on governing boards and finance committees). At this point there is not sufficient research to determine if this pattern will change with a woman pastor. Furthermore, there has not been any research that would indicate any appreciable difference between the performance of a male pastor and a female pastor.

There are indications, however, that women clergy are encountering more opposition from lay women than from men. There are three possible explanations for this. The clergywoman may be perceived as a sexual competitor by some women church members. The clergywoman who is a feminist may encounter hostility from laywomen who do not share her militancy and thus perceive her attitude as a putdown of their roles as wives and mothers. Laywomen may also see the woman pastor's career as something they would have liked to pursue had there been such opportunities when they were considering careers. They now express their dissatisfaction with themselves by antagonism toward the clergywoman.

WHAT KINDS OF JOBS?

Are ordained women being employed in positions that are comparable to those being offered to men with similar training and experience? Unfortunately, data to provide a definitive answer to this question is not yet available. Indications are that women clergy are able to find positions as pastors and on local church staffs if they are able to relocate and do not have too many personal conditions, such as spouses' occupations, type of community or region, or church size. Because the vast majority of church positions are in local congregations as pastors or as staff persons, those persons who want specialized ministries may experience difficulty. Seminary officials report a significant number of women students wanting to enter pastoral counseling. Some of these persons may have difficulty locating appropriate positions.

It is difficult to determine the extent of handicaps faced by women as compared to men of the same education and experience. A large number of ordained women are recent seminary graduates, who would normally be serving smaller congregations at this point in their careers. It will be six to ten years before it can be known whether women ministers will be able to secure calls to the larger churches and are chosen for denominational executive positions.

THE ALMOST-IMPOSSIBLE DREAM

In the mid-1970s the clergy couple, in which both partners are ordained and intent on pursuing ministerial careers, appeared on the church scene. The number of clergy couples is relatively small but is increasing rapidly. The clergy couple is both an old and a new phenomenon in Protestantism. It is old in the sense that the clergyman and his wife have traditionally worked as a team in the local church. Many ministers' wives have exercised significant if informal leadership in the congregations served by their husbands. Such women have acquired considerable expertise in the performance of ministry, although they may not have had formal training or credentials. What is new about the clergy couple is that the wife is now securing the required education and is being ordained; she is thus qualified to pursue a career in the ministry either in conjunction with her husband or separately. And rather than doing so as an unpaid volunteer, she is seeking to do so as a paid professional.

There are three factors that must be considered in the employment of a clergy couple: the husband's career, the wife's career, and the marriage relationship. Three patterns have developed to accommodate the clergy couple.

In the first pattern each partner secures a position as pastor of a church within commuting distance of the other. The couple may reside in one of the parsonages or in both (i.e., staying in each house certain days of the week). The husband and wife have separate employers and make the necessary adjustments in their marriage relationships to do the work required by their respective positions.[3]

A second method is for the couple to accept a position as copastors of a congregation. They share what had been one position and one salary, in effect each taking a half-time job. The specific responsibilities each carries are worked out with the congregation and will depend on the needs of the church, and the skills and interest of the pastors.

The third pattern is a variation of the second. The couple receives a position that is more than one full-time job but less than two. For example, a clergy couple replaced a full-time minister, and a part-time retired pastor who had been serving as parish visitor. Another couple was assigned to six small rural churches that had been served by one part-time and one full-time pastor.

Many clergy couples are young and have limited experience. Assignments to small churches are considered appropriate. The large number of small congregations has maximized employment opportunities; nevertheless, placement has not been easy. The greatest problems have been in those cases where each person wanted his/her own church. It has been necessary not only to find two nearby churches suitable to each partner's skills and experience, but churches willing to call or accept the two particular applicants.

The mobility of clergy couples is proving to be exceedingly difficult. One partner may wish or be forced to relocate; the other may find it inappropriate to do so. Furthermore, the problem of finding two churches in the same area that are ready to employ both pastors greatly increases as one attempts to move to larger congregations.

There are probably enough one-pastor churches that will employ a clergy couple, paying only one salary to both, to provide employment for those couples willing to accept such an arrangement. The number of places, particularly rural circuits, favorably disposed to employ two persons for slightly more than one salary provides additional opportunities. Few congregations large enough to afford two or more full-time staff persons have been inclined to hire clergy couples. They may want other combinations of skills than the couple possesses. More important, staff positions are often avidly sought. The large church can select its staff from a large pool of applicants and does not have to adjust to the needs or desires of either the individual minister or the clergy couple.

The general consensus of denominational officials is that the church simply cannot provide for both the parallel ministerial careers and the marriages of clergy couples. As one national church official stated, "Clergy couples are definitely not the ministerial wave of the future." The couples themselves are facing some difficult choices. They must determine what priority they will give to the performance of ministry, to upward mobility in their professional careers, and to their marriages and families.

One strategy is for the clergy couple to decide that one spouse's career will have priority. It can be either the husband's or the wife's. This person will accept the promotions; the other partner will go along and take whatever position happens to be available. Such a course gives the high priority to the career of one partner and to the couple's marriage. The other partner's career will take second place.

A second strategy is for the couple to give high priority to performing ministry and to their marriage, and low priority to upward mobility. A couple that serves one church and shares one salary would fall into this group. Wife and husband can have an effective shared ministry but reduce the chance of their being called to a large prestigious church or otherwise advancing their careers.

Finally, partners can give high priority to their careers and to upward mobility in the profession, with the result that their marriage may be jeopardized or sacrificed. The husband and wife who serve churches a considerable distance apart and see each other infrequently are an example.

Denominational officials report a high rate of marriage failure among clergy couples. Although the failure rate is high for all marriages, that clergy couple marriages have difficulties should not be surprising. A pastor becomes deeply involved in the congregation and the community. If husband and wife serve two different churches, each is involved with a separate group of people. Irregular hours and being on call seven days a week put a strain on the marriage. If the partners serve the same congregation, they may find themselves in competition with each other. Tensions among church staff members are common. When the church staff is a clergy couple, additional tension may result.

The immediate future will see a continued increase in the number of people seeking both ordination and ministerial careers. There are more women seminarians than ever before, and some ministers' wives are qualifying for ordination.

Clergy couples can have both effective ministries and successful marriages if they are realistic about the potentials and the hazards. The church can, in most instances, provide an opportunity for the clergy couple to engage in ministry. It cannot assure two parallel careers, including equal opportunities for promotion. The clergy couple faces a situation not unlike persons in other professions who are attempting to combine marriage, possibly a family, and two careers. When the requirements of each come into conflict, as they inevitably will, the couple must determine which shall be given priority—what, to them, is most important. If something is to be sacrificed, the couple must make that decision as well.

POSSIBLE CONSEQUENCES

The growing number of ordained women in a period of clergy oversupply will have several effects on the church and the clergy. Indications are that women will constitute a substantial proportion of the total number of candidates for the ministry (possibly between one fourth and one third). To predict the long-term impact of this phenomenon would, of course, be speculation. However, it does seem that the growing number of ordained women will have the greatest effect on the denominational structure, particularly those denominations that carry responsibility for assisting women in securing positions in local churches. In all probability the impact of the women on local congregations will be minimal. The woman pastor's effectiveness will depend on her gifts and competence, as is already the case for her male counterpart. The impact on both the denominations and the local churches of a substantial increase in the number of women pastors will most likely be far less than militant feminists anticipate and traditionalists fear.

Indications are that this increase is affecting the denominations in several ways. Liberal denominations, such as the United Church of Christ, are attracting the largest number of women. A significant number of women ministerial candidates also appears to be gravitating toward denominations with a closed system of clergy placement, such as The United Methodist Church. They are not being recruited by the denomination; rather, the candidates are choosing this system because they see a personal advantage in this method of placement. For example, if a woman can be ordained and admitted to a United Methodist annual conference, the bishop is required to appoint her to a local church or to some other appropriate position. She does not have to seek a call from a congregation. This trend has caused concern among denominational officials, who admit that they do not see where they are going to find positions for all the present and potential women ministers. This could force basic changes in the United Methodist practice of guaranteed appointments for the clergy. The decision regarding pastoral employment may shift from the bishop to the local congregation.

Another potential impact of the larger number of women clergy may be to change the nature of the regional judicatory from a kind of brotherhood to a professional association. Pastors and their families have tended to develop close friendships with other clergy families in the same judicatory. Some friendships begin in college and seminary, and continue throughout the individuals' lives. The ministerial members of some regional judicatories have traditionally referred to themselves as "The Brotherhood." However, the judicatories have been moving toward being more of a professional association and away from a brotherhood idea. One reason is that as they have become larger (chiefly through mergers), the individual member can now know only a small proportion of his or her colleagues. Also both male and female dynamics will likely make the relationship between men clergy and women clergy more formal than when the organization had an all-male membership.

A possible further result of the entrance of a large number of women into the clergy in a period of oversupply may be to depress ministers' salaries. A congregation that is not inclined to call a woman pastor may be willing to do so if she will accept a salary significantly lower than a man. The single woman, or the married woman with an employed husband may be able to underbid the married man with a family. This, of course, is completely contrary to the concept of equal pay for equal work and is an anathema to many people. Nevertheless, in a tight job market if the choice is between a position at a lower salary and no position, some individuals will accept less compensation in order to get the job.

The married clergywoman with an employed husband may feel less pressure to push for salary increases. If the combined family income is high, the congregation may be unwilling to raise the minister's salary.

A final consequence of the growing number of women pastors is that competition between them and their male colleagues probably will increase. As yet, there are relatively few women in each regional judicatory. Many are young and serve small congregations. As time passes and women are in competition for promotions to larger churches, tension between the two groups will increase. This can already be noted in seminary student bodies, where tension exists between some of the militant feminists and the male students. The degree of competition and tension between men clergy and women clergy will be in direct ratio to the scarcity of available positions in the church.

Chapter 6

The Impact on the Church System

A change in the supply of ministers and the demand for their services influences the parts of the church system in different ways and in varying degrees. This chapter is concerned with the manner in which the present clergy job situation is influencing three parts of the church system. The first is the local church; the second, the regional judicatories; and the third, the theological seminaries.

THE LOCAL CHURCH

As the institutions that employ most of the ordained clergy, local churches are obviously influenced by an oversupply of ministers. However, the impact on the congregations is much less drastic than on the clergy, the judicatories, or the theological seminaries. The local church tends to be the most stable unit in the denomination. It is probably least influenced by the latest theological trends or the organizational form adopted by the judicatory. Congregations will experience the effects of the clergy surplus primarily at the time they are seeking a new pastor.

Increased Congregational Options

The perceived shortage of ministers existed for so long a time that most church members are still unaware of how much the situation has changed. Call committees from even medium-sized congregations are amazed and a bit overwhelmed at the large number of applications they now receive. It is not uncommon for a church that is not one of the denomination's prestige pulpits to have a hundred ministers apply. Call committees in some large churches may receive between 200 and 300 clergy dossiers. A United Church of Christ congregation in rural New England, with approximately 150 members, was overwhelmed to receive thirty-five applications for their vacant pulpit. The salary range for the position was between $7,500 and $9,000.

A large pool of applicants increases the options for the congregation. It will almost certainly increase the call committee's sense of power, knowing that a large number of persons are seeking the job. Inevitably, some able ministers will be overlooked or rejected on the basis of superficial criteria simply because the number of applicants must be narrowed down. Committee members may even feel immobilized by the wide choice open to them. One judicatory official likened the situation to children in a candy shop, frustrated because they can choose only one piece out of many.

The clergy oversupply has had an impact on the relationship between congregation and pastor. Higher expectations are being expressed at the time the pastor is employed. For example, church members are insisting on better preaching. Their tolerance for a shabby performance in the pulpit or a retreaded six-year-old sermon is low. The long-term result is that congregations will hold their clergy more accountable for their effectiveness than has been the case in the recent past. This can be a positive experience, where laity and clergy work out criteria and methods for evaluation and support of each other's ministries.

Longer Pastorates

An oversupply of clergy will lead to long pastorates in the same congregation, particularly in those denominations where the minister has tenure in the local church. Because it is harder for a clergyperson to move, he or she may, of necessity, stay in the same place. However, in those denominations where pastors do not have tenure in the congregations, members may be reluctant to retain an unpopular or less competent pastor, particularly if they are aware that a replacement is readily available.

The impact of longer pastorates will be mixed. For some churches and ministers the results will be positive. The pastor may settle down and develop the local church, without having an eye trained on the next move. Issues that might have been avoided by a move will be worked through. In other instances the inability of a minister to move may be a negative experience, as an impasse develops between pastor and people. This makes both continuing education and support groups for clergy imperative.

An Advantage for Small-membership Churches

As stated earlier, the oversupply of clergy may be a boon to churches of small membership. Some of these churches have had to be satisfied with untrained, inexperienced, or part-time leadership. With fewer positions available some ordained persons who might have turned down calls from small churches or a circuit are more willing to accept such calls or appointments. As innovative tentmaking options are developed, this will be even more likely to occur.

The result of the present situation could be that in the period ahead, the church of small membership will have better-qualified clergy than it has had in the past half century. Furthermore, if these congregations can manage to provide both psychic rewards and a reasonable level of material income, they may be able to retain their pastors longer than has been the custom. The larger number of clergy could produce a kind of renaissance for the church of small membership.

Pressure to Hire Women

The increase in the number of ordained women has resulted in pressure on local churches to employ women. This comes from denominational women's advocacy groups and from judicatory placement officials who are required to place women clergy—or feel morally obligated to do so.

However, the congregation that is attractive to the potential minister also has a large number of applicants when it becomes open. Members may feel less compelled to respond positively to the pressure to hire a woman pastor when they realize they are in a "buyer's market." This situation may result in increased tension between the judicatory placement offices and the local churches. In final analysis the decision will be made by the congregation.

Sharing the Pastor

For years it has been a common pattern for many ministers to serve two or more churches, usually small congregations in rural areas. This has been done primarily out of economic necessity, but also because many small congregations do not require the services of a minister full time. Because not every church is able to employ a full-time pastor, they must share one. No doubt the system of congregations sharing a minister will continue for the indefinite future.

The difference made by a clergy oversupply is that churches increasingly have the option of sharing their pastor, not with a nearby congregation, but with a secular job in which the minister is employed. For some congregations it is simply not convenient—or sometimes possible—to find a nearby church with which to share a pastor. The only alternative is to allow or encourage pastors to secure secular jobs and to serve the church on a part-time basis. The benefits and liabilities in this pattern are considered in chapter 9.

THE REGIONAL JUDICATORIES

An oversupply of clergy is putting considerable strain on the regional judicatories (the presbytery, synod, annual conference, classis, and so on). These are the church bodies that, in most denominations, admit persons into the ordained ministry, as well as assist them in securing positions. This section presents some of the ways the changing supply and demand is influencing these bodies.

Clergy Evaluation

Judicatories are being forced to think about some type of clergy evaluation. This is not universal, but some judicatories have been experimenting with various methods, including the development of forms to be used by the minister in a self-evaluation process and by the church members to rate the performance of their minister. It is not clear how the results of these evaluations are being used, or whether they are influencing clergy assignments or promotions. But they do put pressure on the clergy to improve their skills and performance.

Related to clergy evaluation is an increased emphasis on continuing education. Denominations are not only providing more opportunities for continuing education, they (and increasingly congregations) are providing funds for pastors who take courses and participate in training experiences. Pressure is exerted by some judicatories by requiring pastors to report periodically on what they have done in continuing education.

Termination of Ministers

Clergy evaluation can be a step toward the termination of incompetent persons. A result of having more pastors than parishes is increased pressure to terminate those who are unemployable in the church. This is already taking place as some judicatories, which have not expelled ministers in decades except for moral or criminal reasons, have recently terminated some for incompetence.

Whether or not an individual is terminated for incompetence will depend on the denomination's understanding of the relationship between ordination and employment. If the church does not require its clergy to be in clearly definable ministerial positions and is not required to place them in such jobs, it is not necessary to terminate ineffective persons. They are responsible for their own employment, either in the religious or the secular field. The individual who cannot secure a parish or other ministry position must find some other job. This is the case with most denominations that have congregational polities.

In contrast, the denomination that ties ordination to employment as a pastor or some other ministerial position, such as the Lutheran Church in America, cannot permit ordained persons to hold secular jobs. Thus, ministers who are unacceptable as pastors of a congregation and/or cannot find appropriate church positions within the required time have their ordination revoked and are returned to lay status. This is an unambiguous relationship, but it may be a traumatic process for those involved. The transition is made somewhat easier by exit counseling and other termination benefits provided by the denomination.

Lower Retirement Age

One of the ways more positions can be made available quickly is to lower the mandatory retirement age for the clergy. The trend in recent years has been to permit and/or require clergy and other employees to retire at an earlier age. It is uncertain if this will change to follow the national trend toward later mandatory retirement.

90

The problem is the increased burden that lowering the time of retirement places on the denominational pension funds, particularly in a period when such funds are suffering from inflation. The probability is that a person who retires at sixty-two will collect a pension for a longer period of time than someone who stops working at sixty-eight. Denominations are caught between conflicting goals. The desire to have clergy retire early and thus open up jobs conflicts with the need to provide adequate pensions. The strain that is already on the pension funds will probably offset the pressure to lower the retirement age.

Formal and Informal Systems of Clergy Placement

While clergy placement is handled quite differently in various denominations, the regional judicatory has been a key organization. Each denomination has formal procedures for the deployment process; however, there are also informal procedures and networks that play an important role. In a time when positions are in short supply, the informal system takes on added importance. It is advantageous for the ministerial candidate and the pastor wishing to move to be part of the "old boy" network, or what some refer to as the "cousin network." Insiders always have an advantage over outsiders. A pastor who is well known in the region will be more likely to come to the attention of churches seeking pastors. As previously noted, this informal system does not yet work well for women.

An interesting conflict at this point in time is between the informal placement systems and the increasing attempt in many church organizations to give anyone an opportunity to apply for any position. Job openings are advertised with greater frequency. The Episcopal Church circulates a list of vacant parishes, with such information as membership size, availability of a rectory, salary, and type of community. Other denominations publish similar vacancy lists, although some leave it to the clergy to discover openings through informal channels.

Technology has made it possible for congregations to secure information regarding a much larger number of clergy candidates than was the case not too long ago. Computerized systems are utilized by several major denominations to provide data about available clergy to inquiring congregations. As congregations become more precise in identifying their needs, the computer systems are able to provide lists of clergy that match these needs. Although there has been resistance to such "impersonal" methods, these systems have provided congregations and clergy with wider options. Other technology has greatly broadened the base of placement; for example, photocopiers make it easy to send a local church a copy of a minister's entire file, including his or her service record, transcript, letters of recommendation, and so forth. Obviously, the impact of such technology on the deployment system has been considerable.

Technology will tend to favor those outside the old-boy network. It can bring such persons to the attention of the employing agency and give them opportunities for consideration that would have been highly unlikely. But the informal system will probably still be the most important factor in determining who secures the position, especially in a time of oversupply.

Support System

Oversupply, with its negative impact on clergy morale, is bringing increased pressures on the regional judicatories and the national denominations to provide support systems for clergy. This involves much more than the occasional continuing education course, a spiritual life retreat, or even an increase in salary and fringe benefits. It includes assistance in career assessment and counseling, better communications between denominational officials and the clergy, helpful support of the minister's family, and as one judicatory report states, "supportive groups to help overcome the loneliness of the ministry."

THE THEOLOGICAL SEMINARIES

The present oversupplied job market has heightened the long-standing tension between the seminary and the church. Schools of theology are finding themselves in a kind of cross fire between expectations and needs of students, denominations, and local churches, and other functions of the seminaries, such as graduate education and theological research. Calls for increased accountability are growing. Local congregations employ the vast majority of seminary graduates. Judicatory leaders and pastors recruit candidates for the ministry and are influential in determining which seminaries individuals will attend. Furthermore, denominations and their constituent congregations provide a not-inconsiderable portion of the financial support necessary for the operation of the schools of theology. At the same time, many denominationally affiliated seminaries are independent of direct church control. While the degree of autonomy varies by denomination, this independence may heighten the tension between denominations and seminaries, especially in responding to an oversupply of clergy.

Relationship with Students

If a student anticipates difficulty in finding a position upon graduation, she or he may feel that the seminary is not providing adequate preparation. While the real problem may be the job shortage and not the educational program, the school may nevertheless be the recipient of the student's anger, caused by anxiety over the perceived lack of job opportunities. This may take the form of antagonism directed against the faculty and the administration. It may result, for example, in a movement to revise the curriculum to make it less "academic" and more relevant to the practice of ministry.

If the problem is lack of jobs, a change in the curriculum can have little impact other than perhaps giving the graduate of a particular school a competitive advantage. This assumes the revised curriculum has enabled the seminarian to acquire the skills that make her or him more acceptable to a call committee.

Student Recruitment

Seminaries may encounter increasing difficulties in recruiting and maintaining their present level of enrollment. It is generally assumed that persons who elect a career in the church do so for reasons other than material rewards. Thus an individual who has a "call to preach" is expected to respond positively, regardless of the job openings for a seminary graduate. However, persons enter the ministry for a variety of complex reasons and with different degrees of commitment. Some whose commitment to the ministry is marginal will probably seek careers in other fields if they perceive limited opportunities for employment. Then these persons will not be potential seminary students, and the pool of applicants will shrink.

Students that we interviewed reported feeling pressure to attend a school related to their own church in order to increase their chances of employment. The pressure may be self-generated. By attending a denominational seminary, students feel they have more opportunities to become acquainted with church leaders who may remember them when job openings occur. As one student who was reluctantly transferring put it, "As a graduate of _____ Seminary, I'll be more visible to congregations seeking pastors." Also the pressure may come from the denominations that want more control over their clergy.

Denominational pressure is apparent in the increasing number of denominationally related courses that are being required of students. This puts nondenominational seminaries at a disadvantage when they are required to provide an increasing range of required courses for the various denominations represented among their students. In some instances, officials of nondenominational seminaries acknowledged recruitment problems stemming from these denominational pressures. However, some of the more conservative or evangelically oriented nondenominational seminaries seem to be having little trouble drawing students, including those from mainline denominations (see Appendix, Table 6, where much of the increase in inter- and nondenominational enrollments can be traced to the more evangelically oriented schools). For example, approximately 45 percent of United Presbyterian seminary students under the care of presbytery are not in United Presbyterian seminaries. One person interviewed referred to Fuller (a nondenominational seminary) as "the second largest Presbyterian seminary in the nation."

Relationship with Denominations

The clergy surplus is creating strained relationships between seminaries and denominations. In addition to complaints about inadequate professional training, some church leaders feel that the schools are producing too many ministerial candidates, thus putting the judicatories in the embarrassing position of having to reject some applicants for ordination. One way this situation can be avoided is for the seminaries to graduate fewer persons. This desire for fewer

94

graduates was expressed by a member of a judicatory screening committee to a seminary professor: "I wish your faculty would give more Fs."

Some schools have taken steps to limit enrollment. A few Episcopal schools are requesting applicants to have their bishop's endorsement. One seminary will accept only two new students each year from each diocese. The president of a United Methodist related school of theology stated, "Our commitment is to fewer but better students."

If denominational leaders perceive that an oversupply of clergy will continue over a long period, there will be reluctance to continue financial support for theological seminaries. Pressures to reduce—or at least not to increase—the level of support will be felt. The need for the present number of schools will be questioned, and attempts to close or merge some can be anticipated. During the 1968-72 quadrennium The United Methodist Church had a special committee that studied its fourteen schools of theology and recommended a sharp reduction in number. Since 1972 the total has been reduced by one, as two institutions merged. Consideration also has been given to merging two others.

Strains develop as there are conflicts of interest between the schools of theology and their parent denominations. Seminaries need students and financial support. If the denominations cannot employ the graduates, they will be reluctant to provide funds and might see the reduction in the number of schools as a logical way of relieving both the financial pressure and the embarrassment of having more clergy than vacant positions.

Part III

Coping with the Job Situation

Chapter 7

Rethinking Ordination

In *The Green Pastures* there is a scene in which the Lord tells Noah that everything that is nailed down is coming loose.[1] That is an appropriate description of the present situation with regard to clergy employment in several of the denominations we have studied. While it overstates the case to say that everything about clergy employment is coming loose, there are clearly quite a number of loose boards. Our research has documented several of them: increasing numbers of clergy without employment; a growing number wanting to change positions but unable to do so; more seminarians, especially women; declining church membership in several denominations; strained economic resources; and a growing number of small congregations that cannot afford full-time pastors.

This kind of a situation creates a crisis in the church. By crisis we don't mean a threat of imminent demise, but its literal meaning as a decisive time, a time for making judgments about possible directions for the future. The open systems perspective, which we have found useful in our analysis, holds that systems have the capacity for self-renewal and can maintain themselves by self-initiated change. They can respond positively to a period of crisis.

Self-renewal is not easy, however. Old patterns of functioning are hard to alter; the assumptions, tacit or explicit, on which the patterns rest are resistant to reexamination and change. Various parts of the system (for example, theological seminaries and local congregations) are often relatively autonomous. Despite these difficulties, we believe that self-renewal is the appropriate response to the present.

In this chapter we begin our concern for self-renewal by focusing

99

on the meaning of ministry, especially in relation to ordination. We draw on New Testament views of ministry to question some current assumptions about ordination that block self-renewal. In subsequent chapters we focus on other responses to the clergy oversupply that can also contribute to self-renewal.

NEW TESTAMENT PERSPECTIVES

In considering assumptions relative to ordination and ministry, we have been driven back to a study of the historical development of ministry, especially during the New Testament period. While we do not propose a return to New Testament practices—that would be historically and sociologically naive—we do take quite seriously the orientation to ministry that is evident in New Testament documents. As a background to questioning some of the current assumptions about ministry, we note briefly some of the major aspects of the New Testament perspective.

What seems to be fundamental in the New Testament is that ministry is not a term descriptive of an office or position within the church. Ministry (*diakonia*) is rather the service to both God and neighbor to which all Christians are called by virtue of their baptism. The locus classicus for this understanding is in the first letter of Peter: "You are a chosen race, a royal priesthood, a holy nation, God's own people, that you may declare the wonderful deeds of him who called you out of darkness into his marvelous light. Once you were no people but now you are God's people; once you had not received mercy but now you have received mercy [2:9-10]." There is no priesthood in the New Testament church save the priesthood of all believers, who are called to share in the priestly ministry of Jesus Christ. A set-apart official priesthood as a special group within the church did not develop until considerably later.[2] Nor was it until later, when an ordained ministry had developed, that distinctions were made between types of calls to the ministry; while all Christians were seen as called to discipleship, some were especially called to become ordained ministers.[3] In the beginning there was one calling in which all Christians shared.

The act that dramatizes this calling is baptism. Although baptism has too often been relegated to a name-giving, dedicatory event, it may more appropriately be thought of as incorporation into the ministry of Jesus Christ (Mark 10:38-39). It is the commissioning of every Christian, in which one is called to use one's distinctive gifts for the service of God in the world. In the traditions that practice infant baptism, followed by confirmation at an older age, the latter event becomes the occasion for acknowledging or confirming this calling to ministry.

What, then, of special ministries within the church? Are there no distinctions? Clearly, there were diverse services within the early church that recognized the differing gifts of various members (1 Corinthians 12:4ff. and Ephesians 4:4ff.). But these do not appear to have been viewed as formal offices or positions in distinction from the ministry of the whole church. Nor did greater honor adhere to some gifts and services in contrast to others. That there were efforts to make some gifts and services distinctive and to confer higher status to them is clear from Paul's words to the Corinthians; however, the norm Paul held out for them was that of a diversity of interdependent gifts and services within the one calling to ministry.

As the church grew in size and complexity, and as it had to come to terms with both its Jewish heritage and the various religious movements of its Graeco-Roman environment, certain distinctive functions of ministry began to emerge and become regularized. Early on, the apostles were understood to be a special group. As ones who had encountered the risen Christ and had been commissioned by him to proclaim his resurrection, the apostles had distinctive status and function in the early church, but this status could not be passed on to successors. As witnesses to the resurrection they were unique. It was their message—the core of the tradition—and not their office that was passed on.[4]

In addition to the apostles, other functions of ministry came to be recognized in the various churches, although there was no uniformity. Paul's list in 1 Corinthians 12:28 includes prophets, teachers, miracle-workers, healers, helpers, administrators, and speakers in tongues. Elsewhere, evangelists and pastors are mentioned, as are bishops, deacons, and deaconesses. The "bishops," however, were not bishops in the later, more formal sense of the word, but rather were persons designated to preside over community functions, especially community meals. There were also

101

presbyters or elders (from whom the bishops were often chosen), persons with acknowledged wisdom and maturity in the faith, who formed a council to guide and oversee the community in its ministry. Each of these ministries appears to have been functionally defined, and persons exercized the ministries according to their particular gifts or charisms. The ministries were not offices or positions in any formal organizational sense.[5]

It was not long before the church was led to develop more formal patterns of ministry, including institutionalized positions or offices. Both the needs of a church growing in size and complexity and the need to remain faithful to the central elements of the gospel in the face of heretical movements led to the establishment of more regularized patterns of church order. Such a development was a practical and sociological necessity for the sake of the church's mission. It is important to emphasize, nevertheless, that order developed for these reasons instead of adherence to a divinely legitimated model.[6] Only later would theological justifications be advanced to legitimate the patterns that developed. Rather, there was in the early centuries of the church's life a remarkable freedom under the leading of the Spirit to create new ministries to meet the emerging needs of the growing, geographically diverse communities of faith.

To be sure, as more fixed patterns of church order were institutionalized, the freedom and flexibility of the earlier period were limited. While some limitation was inevitable, institutionalization brought its problems. As time passed the patterns became rigid and resistant to change. They had to be challenged as Christians sought to respond in faithfulness to God under the guidance of the Holy Spirit in new settings and circumstances. This tension between order and freedom, whether with reference to the ministry or to other aspects of church life, has been a major motif of church history. It remains a major tension currently, as will be evident as we consider several taken-for-granted assumptions about ministry that need to be questioned in light of the current situation.

In turning to these assumptions, it may be helpful to summarize the major points of this brief foray into the early church's perspective on ministry: (1) all Christians were called to ministry; (2) there were a variety of functions of ministry within the one Body of Christ that Christians, by virtue of their gifts, were called to exercise for the good of the community; (3) as the church grew in size and complexity these ministries, of necessity, became more formalized and ordered; (4) the functions of ministry and the patterns into which they were ordered were subject to change as the church followed the Spirit's leading in changing circumstances and contexts for ministry. What, then, are some of the assumptions about ordination that we believe need to be questioned?

ASSUMPTIONS ABOUT ORDINATION

Real Ministry Is Ordained Ministry

Hardly a new assumption is one that views authentic ministry to be that carried out by ordained persons. The ministry of laypersons is perceived to be of lesser value and status. To be sure, such an assumption is not part of the official theology of ministry of most denominations. In principle, most denominations acknowledge the New Testament insistence that ministry belongs to the whole people, lay and ordained. Ordination is typically viewed primarily as ensuring, for reasons of good order, that the task of equipping all the ministers (the whole people of God) is carried out by persons judged to have the necessary gifts and training. The difference between ordained and lay ministers, then, is officially one of function, not of substance and status. Nevertheless, it is not difficult to discover examples of the tacit acceptance of status differences between the ministry of ordained and of lay Christians. If, for example, a layperson gets serious about her or his faith commitment, a typical response is to encourage her or him to "go into the ministry," by which is meant attend seminary and become ordained. It is assumed that one who is really serious about the faith must be called to ordained ministry. This mystique about ordination is one of the possible causes for the increase in entrants into seminary in recent years.

There are at least two contributors to this mystique. First, there is the quite ancient belief that ordination confers, or recognizes, a higher degree of spirituality or sanctity. In the early centuries of the church's history, possibly as late as the fourth century, there do not seem to have been distinctions made between the spirituality of clergy and of laity. Leaders of the church, ordained or not, were viewed as primus inter pares, first ministers among equals in spirituality as in other qualities. As such they could point to themselves as examples that all Christians should follow, even as they followed Christ's example. "Be imitators of me, as I am of Christ [1Cor. 11:1]," Paul wrote to the Corinthians.

By late in the fourth century a hierarchical understanding of the ministry developed under Neoplatonic influences, in which it was believed that degrees of exemplary sanctity were attached to the offices of ministry (for example, bishops, priests, and deacons) according to rank. Bishops had the highest rank and therefore were the most spiritual and so on down the ladder. Added to this was the developing monastic tradition with its ascetic ideal, which became the defining characteristic of the exemplary sanctity presumed to be inherent in the ministerial office as contrasted with the lay status. As Roman Catholic historian and theologian Bernard Cooke puts it:

> What this means among other things is that the clergy became increasingly a separate class in Christian society; they were not "ordinary people." They were above the laity not just in the dignity of their functions within the community but in the very nature of their membership in the church.[7]

The other contributor to the clergy-lay distinction is more recent in origin. It is the impact of the professionalization of ministry. Ordination is increasingly tied to attaining professional competence, usually through training of an extended sort, that enables a person to perform certain functions judged to be important. Thus far, there is no problem. Competent clergy, that is, professional clergy, are clearly needed to equip the people of God for their ministry. There is no virtue in inflicting an incompetent, untrained clergyperson on a congregation! But the move to ensure competence in the ordained has often been subtly converted into professionalism, an ideology that exalts the professional (ordained) status vis-à-vis the laity, creating differences of prestige and power in the church and hindering the mutual ministry of the whole people of God. Therefore, if one wants to become a real minister, he or she must attain professional (ordained) status.

We do not propose that ordained clergy are not needed or that professional competence is not important for those who are ordained. Our reading of the history and theology of the ministry and our experience in the church suggest the opposite. For reasons of right order and for equipping the people of God for the exercise of their ministry, persons with the requisite gifts and competence are needed. But we believe this *functional* necessity is the rationale for ordination, not the creation of a spiritual elite or a professional caste. Real ministry is the mutual ministry of the whole people of God, lay and ordained.

Indelible Orders—*Even* for Protestants?

In Graham Greene's novel *The Power and the Glory* the central character is a priest who is an alcoholic and the father of an illegitimate child. He is fleeing for his life on a charge of treason. He is captured, and he says to his captor, "It doesn't matter so much my being a coward—and all the rest. I can put God into a man's mouth just the same—and I can give him God's pardon. It wouldn't make any difference to that if every priest in the Church was like me."[8] The priest's words reflect a highly consequential view of the ordained ministry that goes back to Augustine, in the late fourth and early fifth centuries. It was he who articulated the concept of the validity of the sacraments, *ex opere operato,* regardless of the personal behavior of the priest who celebrated them. Through ordination an indelible *character dominicus* (priestly character) was given the ordained; he was ordained for life. As church historian George H. Williams has noted, this had the additional consequence of making "ordination wholly a permanent possession of the individual apart from the community in which and through which it was conferred."[9] Such a change undercuts the corporate view of ministry as belonging to the whole Body of Christ that had been prevalent from New Testament times. Among Protestants, The Episcopal Church retains the view of ordination as conferring a lifetime, indeed eternal, status, although the indelibility of the orders has not always been emphasized.

The doctrine of indelible orders has been much criticized within and outside of Catholicism. Luther, for example, explicitly repudiated it and agreed that the ordained ministry made sense only in relation to a congregation that had called a person to be its pastor. Ordination thus became the confirmation of a person's call to the pastoral ministry, especially the call from a particular congregation, and of the person's fitness to respond to that call. American Protestants, who were much influenced by the evangelical awakenings, came to be particularly concerned about an individual's fitness for ministry, especially one's faith and piety. If the clergy's primary task was to lead others to conversion, then he or she must also be a converted and exemplary person.

In spite of the rejection both of the belief in indelible orders and of the separation of ordination from the call of the community, Protestants generally have not followed the full logic of their beliefs; that is, they have not always tied ordination solely to the call from a congregation (or other ecclesiastical agency) or required reordination when one moves from one congregation or church position to another. Rather, once the initial call has been extended (or in the case of United Methodists, once the person has been accepted into membership in an annual conference, which is that denomination's equivalent of an ecclesiastical call), the person is ordained only once. There are no subsequent ordinations upon receiving a new call, nor is there any requirement for a periodic renewal of ordination vows. Further, with some exceptions (for example, some Lutheran bodies), it is generally possible for a clergyperson to retain her or his ordained status indefinitely, even where there is no congregational or extracongregational ecclesiastical position in which one is functioning. The large number of clergy functioning in secular (nonchurch) occupations is an example. They retain their ordination without an ecclesiastical call. In recent years United Methodists have designated such clergy as "ministers to society," which is a way of "assigning" them a call. Thus, even though indelible ordination is not ascribed to and the significance of ordination as confirming one's call is emphasized, the practice of a once-for-all-time ordination and of typically retaining one's ordination in the absence of an ecclesiastical call makes Protestant ordination functionally similar in many respects to the traditional Catholic teaching. Ordination for Protestants, if not indelible, is explicitly or tacitly assumed to be a lifetime status.

There are reasons for this that have little or no direct relation to ordination. One such reason is the assumption, as in most professions, that a professional role, such as the clergy role, is one that is pursued as a career over a lifetime. Further, there is the requirement of a lengthy and costly educational process that one does not undertake lightly. As important as both these factors are in contributing to a clergyperson's sense of lifetime commitment to the ordained ministry, they do not adequately account for the considerable anguish and guilt that clergy often feel when they consider leaving the ordained ministry for a secular occupation. A study of ex-pastors in the United Church of Christ found a sizable minority for whom leaving was a very difficult experience that continued to trouble them after they had made the break.[10] To the expectation of a professional career and the long educational process must be added the impact of the continuing although implicit sense of indelible orders, regardless of the explicit theology of ordination.

Such an assumption, whether tacit or explicit, has important practical consequences in an oversupplied clergy job market. For one thing, it makes the pain even greater for clergy who are unable to secure positions in the church system and therefore unable to fulfill their ordination. Equally as important, this assumption often makes it hard to carry out meaningful performance evaluations. Clergy who are ineffective as pastors or are otherwise unsuited for continued functioning are frequently allowed to remain in the ordained ministry partly because of the implicit assumption of an indelible ordination.

We believe that the assumption of indelible orders needs to be questioned. While a lifetime career as an ordained minister may be the legitimate expectation of most persons who become clergy, it should be made clear that ordination constitutes no irrevocable guarantee. More specifically, we propose the following possibilities: (1) periodic renewal of ordination vows, perhaps every five years, coupled with a meaningful performance review; (2) a recommissioning or renewal of ordination vows when a clergyperson assumes a new position; (3) a requirement of continuing personal and professional development, linked to the performance review, with financial support and time to undertake the necessary study. For those persons whose performance over time indicates that they are not suited for continued functioning as ordained clergy, there should be developed supportive, just, and effective procedures of exiting the ministry with dignity. It is no favor to the clergyperson, to his or her family, to the congregation, or to the mission and ministry of the church to perpetuate ineffective clergy for whatever reason, including an assumption—implicit or otherwise—that ordination confers a lifetime or indelible status.

Real Ministry Is the Ministry of Word, Sacrament, and Order

A final assumption that we believe should be questioned is that real ministry is the ministry of Word and Sacrament, with Order being added in some traditions. This is an ancient view of the primary functions of ministry, based on the threefold ministry of Jesus as prophet, priest, and king. In particular, it reflects the second-century emergence of the distinctive role of the *episkopos* or bishop. Originally designated by the presbyters to preside at the Eucharist, the president gradually took on other functions, such as preaching, teaching, administration, and pastoral care. He became the *episkopos*, or head of the local church. By the end of the third century the concentration of these functions in this office prevailed everywhere. Along with this concentration of functions there developed the doctrine, contrary to the New Testament understanding of ministry, "that a certain priestly power inhered in the office of bishops, who were the successors not only of the Apostles, but also of the Old Testament high priests."[11] As bishops came to preside over multiple congregations, they delegated the performance of most of these functions (and their priestly powers) to a presbyter in each congregation under their care: the bishops and the presbyter-priests constituted the priesthood, with responsiblity for Word, Sacrament, and Order, while other ministers of the church, who performed other functions, were recognized as "lower orders."[12]

This threefold view of the functions of ordained ministry has survived to the present, but there have been differing priorities given to the functions under changing historical circumstances.[13] The sacramental role dominated the perspectives of the Roman Catholic Church throughout most of its history, from John Chrysostom in the fourth century onward. During the Middle Ages, Pope Gregory the Great emphasized the ordering functions, with the minister as pastoral ruler. The Reformation brought to the fore the preaching and catechetical roles of the clergy as servants of the Word, a conception which has dominated evangelical Protestantism since that time.

What have been the effects of restricting ordination to these functions? A generally positive consequence has been to exercise some control over these three central aspects of the church's life. They are too important to be left to chance. Thus the church has typically insisted that persons performing these functions be authorized (ordained) to do so on the basis of requisite gifts (charisms) and training. Again, however, this is for the sake of good order, and as Luther emphasized, persons set aside for carrying out these functions are only doing what each Christian has the power to do by virtue of his or her baptism.

A second, not-so-positive consequence of restricting ordination to Word, Sacrament, and Order has been to relegate other functions of ministry to secondary, if not second-class, status. The eye becomes more important than the hand, the mouth becomes more important than the foot, denying the organic interdependence of the ministry of the whole body in its several parts or functions. We have already commented on this with regard to laity, but it is also true of ordained persons serving in nonparochial settings.

Since the functions of Word, Sacrament, and Order have primary reference to the local church or parish, nonparochial functions of ministry are frequently judged to be of lower status. More than one clergyperson leaving a parish position for a nonparochial one has been chided for "leaving *the* ministry." Such comments are detrimental under any circumstances but are particularly so when there are significant numbers of clergy unable to secure full-time parish or nonparish positions. What lies behind such comments is the implicit if not explicit assumption that *only* the functions of Word, Sacrament, and Order, which are primarily parish related, are *real* ministry.

In light of the current oversupply we have the opportunity to clarify the meaning of ordination in relation to the various functions of ministry. Short of doing away with ordination altogether—a position that we do not support—we see three options open to the churches. The least radical option is to continue to ordain all candidates to a ministry of Word, Sacrament, and Order, regardless of the settings in which they will function or the responsibilities of their positions. This is to take a generalist view of ordination, seeing the three functions as the primary tasks for which ordination gives authority, regardless of setting or position, in contrast to the more general priesthood of all believers.[14] While the option involves no real change from the current practice in most denominations, it necessitates a much greater clarity about the meaning of ordination in relation to nonparochial ministries than currently is the case. Do the three functions constitute representative functions central to all ordained persons, regardless of their responsibilities and settings of ministry? Are they the only functions necessitating ordination?

A second option is to continue to ordain persons only to Word, Sacrament, and Order, and to restrict ordination to those persons who actually perform these three functions as primary and regular tasks of their ministry. Persons engaged in positions in denominational bureaucracies, those like ourselves involved in research and teaching, persons in pastoral counseling centers, and those in a variety of other ministries not directly engaged in proclamation, administering the sacraments, or ordering the life of a congregation would not be ordained. Such persons would relinquish their ordination if they moved from a position involving primary and regular responsibility for Word, Sacrament, and Order to some other position, whether church related or not. This is a carrying out of the logic that ordination is neither indelible nor a lifetime status.

A third option would be to develop types of ordination in addition to Word, Sacrament, and Order. In doing this the church would recognize the several functions of ministry that have evolved as it has developed in differing times and places. This was in part the significance of the diaconate in the early centuries of the church's history. Diaconal ministries were those set apart for various ministries of service within the church and society other than the ministry of Word, Sacrament, and Order. In the medieval period, however, the diaconate came to be viewed as a stepping-stone to ordination to the priesthood (Word, Sacrament, and Order); some traditions have retained a perpetual diaconate as a separate order.

Whatever term would be used to describe persons not functioning primarily and regularly in the ministry of Word, Sacrament, and Order, there would need to be a greater intentionality about the meaning of ordination. Also, there would need to be clarity about those functions believed to be of such importance to the life of the church as to require ordination or some special kind of authorization in recognition of particular gifts and competence. Such functions may or may not be undertaken on a full-time basis and would not necessarily carry a stipend. Furthermore, it would not be assumed that the various ordained ministries were interchangeable, so that a person could move easily from one to another. That would be done only on the basis of a recognized gift (charism) for the ministry in question and the requisite training. We might add that some traditions—for example, the Southern Baptists—already follow such a practice by ordaining some as pastors, some as educators, others as ministers of music, and so on.

We do not wish to promote any one of these options as necessarily being better than the others. Each has merits and deficiencies, both generally and in relation to the current oversupply. Our concern in presenting the options is to question the assumption that *real* ministry is that of Word, Sacrament, and Order, and to call for greater clarity in our understanding of ordination and its purpose within the life of the church.

In this chapter we have considered several of the assumptions about ministry that we believe need to be questioned in light of a theology of ministry and of present trends in the life of the church. It may be that the present trends are the Spirit's way of leading us to rethink our assumptions and to discover anew the one ministry to which both lay and ordained ministers are called. In considering these assumptions we have questioned patterns that are weighted with sacred tradition and have, at one time or another, served the church well. They are also patterns that are heavy in their social status implications, and it may be that social status factors, more than theological ones, will block change in the status quo. We have not tried to present a coherent new set of assumptions about ministry, nor do we see any single pattern emerging. Rather, we believe that the present situation in the church is an opportunity, under the Holy Spirit's leadership, to question old assumptions and develop multiple patterns of ministry, reflecting the ordered diversity that is appropriate for now and for the emerging future.

Chapter 8

Survival Tactics for Clergy

As the person most affected by the changing job market, the minister asks the question, "What can I do to deal effectively with the situation?" Some specific things the individual can do to respond to the oversupply of clergy are the subject of this chapter.

UNDERSTAND THE JOB MARKET

Clergy and the candidates for ordained ministry currently face a situation that is new to this generation of church people. The shortage of pastors persisted over so long a period that many persons are unaware that it no longer exists. Furthermore, a few people are reluctant to admit there is an oversupply of clergy; to do so somehow reflects negatively on the church. Denominational leaders have long told youth that if they would dedicate their talents to the service of the Lord, the church would find places for them. To have to tell applicants that there are no jobs is terribly embarrassing; yet not to prepare them for the situation they face is to do them a disservice.

The candidate who cannot locate a position or the ordained person who is unable to secure a call may feel that it is the result of personal inadequacies. In addition to feelings of frustration, the individual may consider himself or herself a failure. The result can be a kind of despair that causes one to accept defeat prematurely. One may assume that the entire problem lies with him or her. By being aware of what the prospects for positions are, the clergyperson or candidate can have a healthier attitude, knowing that the entire responsibility does not rest on her or him. It is therefore possible to take action that will provide the best chance of securing a position.

REEXAMINE YOUR CALL

An oversupply of clergy leads the clergyperson to reexamine his or her understanding of the call to the ministry. The current situation tends to force the individual to deal again—or perhaps for the first time—with the hard questions of the nature and purpose of the ministry, to consider the theological assumptions that have provided the basis, not only for the decisions relating to a career, but for the course of his or her entire life.

When clergy were in short supply and jobs were easy to come by, a minister could readily avoid such a reexamination of basic beliefs. Activities in the parish consumed as much time as was available. One's career seemed relatively predictable. Even if promotions did not come as frequently as desired, one could serve comfortably within an ecclesiastical system and perhaps avoid raising the tough theological questions. There was always another, possibly better, job in the church system if things didn't go well, or simply if one became bored in the present situation.

Now there may be no other job to which to move, or there may not be one that is desirable. Promotion, or even the possibility of moving to another church, is problematic. To remain in the ordained ministry persons must be convinced that this is where they want to invest their lives. The adverse conditions created by the oversupply will tend to force each person to reexamine his or her call to the ministry to see if it is still valid under the present circumstances. The individual will have to be convinced and remain convinced that the theological underpinnings are sound and will support one's continued commitment to the ministry, particularly when conditions in the church are less predictable and secure.

CONSIDER THE MEANING OF SUCCESS

The clergyperson, and to some extent the entire church, must look critically at what is perceived to be success in the ministry. Clergy and church members to a great degree have accepted the model of success of the larger society, the idea that bigger is better. Thus the successful pastor is perceived to be one who moves from smaller to larger churches, from smaller to larger salaries, from a less desirable community to a more desirable one. The clergy accept this pattern as the model for their careers. They carefully note the churches served by their seminary classmates to determine if they are staying abreast of their peers; they study clergy salaries reported in the denominational yearbooks to see where they are in relation to others.

The unfortunate aspect of all this is that it defines success in the ministry in purely institutional terms. Prestige, status, and income become the chief criteria. Such qualities and characteristics as faithfulness to the gospel, the ability to preach and to extend effective pastoral care to the members of the parish, and the enabling of laypeople in their ministries are ignored in favor of larger memberships and bigger budgets.

The entire church system supports the bigger is better concept. Ministers are urged by denominational executives to persuade their people to contribute more to church causes. The reports that pastors prepare for publication in judicatory yearbooks are quantitative; that is, they call for the number of members and baptisms, and the amount raised for salary, missions, and so forth.

Unless Christian people are able to find measures of success for the ministry that are based on the nature and purpose of the gospel, we can anticipate an increasing number of frustrated and embittered clergy. The denominational system in a period of clergy oversupply is simply not going to be able to provide channels of upward mobility and greater compensation for the pastors who expect to move from smaller to larger churches. The tight job market will limit mobility. A reexamination of the criteria of success in the ministry is a continuing necessity; in a period of clergy oversupply it is crucial.

ACHIEVE A RENEWED SENSE OF CALL

One of the ways in which some clergy have revitalized their ministry has been to move to new congregations. This gives them new groups of people with whom to work and a chance to use the ideas that proved successful in their previous parishes.

Such a strategy does not work well in a time of clergy oversupply, when moving is much more difficult. It is critical therefore that ministers and denominational leaders discover ways that a pastor may achieve a renewed sense of call while remaining in the same parish. This is not an easy task, but one that is vital to the effectiveness of the clergy's work and the ministry of the parish.

The first step in this renewed sense of call is acceptance of the fact that mobility may not be an option. Some ministers find it easier to move than to deal with the difficult issues in particular parishes. In some instances, pastors never really face and deal with problems, because they know that by holding out for a year or two longer, they can move on and leave the situations to their successors. A clergyperson who accepts that he or she will likely have to stay, will be more ready to face troublesome conditions in the parish and work them through to satisfactory solutions. This, however, will necessitate new knowledge and skills and other resources of grace.

It follows, then, that the second important aspect to achieving a renewed sense of calling is continuing growth and development, including personal and spiritual growth, and the pastoral skills necessary for an effective ministry. One cannot minister effectively solely on the basis of what was learned in seminary in preparation for ordination. Seminaries are often targets for criticism that they have not prepared candidates sufficiently for ministry, and some of this criticism is justified. But there is no way the seminary can adequately prepare candidates for effective ministry throughout their careers.

In recent years opportunities for continuing personal and professional development have expanded greatly in quantity and quality. Not only are there a growing number of occasional workshops and courses, but there are degree programs, including the Doctor of Ministry, that offer sustained and structured opportunities for personal and professional development. The most effective of these courses and programs in helping clergy gain a renewed sense of calling are those that provide opportunities for disciplined theological reflection on the practice of one's ministry, development of new pastoral skills, spiritual growth, and the experience of colleague support. Clergy report less interest in and help from programs aimed primarily at updating them on the latest theological scholarship.

Transition points in one's career are especially significant occasions for a systematic focus on personal and professional growth. The first three to five years following graduation from seminary constitute one such point, while the previously mentioned midcareer transition (when one has been in the ministry approximately fifteen to twenty years) is another. The years immediately prior to retirement are a third important transition stage. Needs, interests, and career goals differ from one step to another, and some judicatories and seminaries are beginning to develop special programs of continuing education and peer support with particular transition points in view.[1] A pastor in a program designed for midcareer clergy described what the experience meant to him during a particularly difficult time in his ministry.

> As a direct consequence of my experience with the group: (1) I had a place to stand; (2) I was able to keep a positive and intentional ministry going in spite of all the flack (self-image, though somewhat tarnished, was at least presentable in public); (3) congregational attendance grew, and before you could think, the enemy was surrounded by most of the substantial people. . . . [The group] has also given me new direction, motivation, and purpose in the parish ministry.

Certain obstacles will have to be overcome if one is to develop a systematic plan for continuing education and growth. Not least are time and finances. A national clergy study showed that finances are a particularly serious obstacle to continuing education for clergy in small-membership churches.[2] Increasingly, however, financial assistance is available through judicatories and congregations. Also, some denominations are strongly encouraging congregations to build time for annual continuing education into ministers' contracts. One seminary, with help from a private foundation, has developed a program by which rural pastors (frequently from small churches) can spend a semester in residence. A stipend is provided for the pastor and for a seminary student to serve as interim pastor. Therefore, in various ways, means of overcoming the obstacles of time and financial support for continuing education are being developed. Clergy who wish to keep their ministry fresh and vital in a time of limited mobility will use these growing opportunities for personal and professional development.

In addition to continuing education, the incidence of regular performance evaluation of clergy by both local church and denominational leaders is increasing. While such evaluations can be threatening, they can also be helpful when done in supportive context. Among the positive benefits, performance evaluations provide an opportunity for the pastor to (1) reflect with others in the ministry situation on the meaning of ministry, (2) develop with judicatory and congregational leaders performance criteria appropriate to the job at hand, (3) assess one's strengths and areas of needed growth, (4) get feedback regarding specific areas of performance, and (5) develop a plan for continuing education and growth. Far from being a negative experience, such an evaluation can help the clergyperson achieve a renewed sense of call, with or without relocation, that is vital to a faithful and effective ministry.

ASSESS YOUR STYLE OF MINISTRY

Individuals develop different styles of ministry, depending on a range of complex factors, such as personality, understanding of the nature and purpose of the church, and the expectations of the congregation and the judicatory officials. The current clergy job market should lead the pastor to assess critically his or her style of ministry to determine its effectiveness and appropriateness for the present time.

One aspect of style that is always important, but especially so as clergy find themselves staying longer in congregations, is what may be called religious authenticity. The clergyperson most effective in ministry is the one who conveys in his or her day-to-day relationships and in pastoral performance a humanity grounded in personal faith, an inner strength that allows him or her to be open and vulnerable to others, a piety free of piosity. John Fletcher, in a perceptive article on religious authenticity, describes its opposite—religious inauthenticity—with comments made by laity in interviews about their most serious problems with clergy: "He speaks down to us . . . did not have head and heart together . . . pious . . . hypocritical . . . lost on a mountaintop . . . did not live the gospel in his own life . . . treated the congregation like children . . . could not relate religion and life's problems."[3] Pastors who will have increasingly longer tenures in congregations will find religious authenticity to be a key element of an effective pastoral style. The clergyperson who has it will wear well with a congregation over the long haul. It is not, however, a style that one puts on like a set of clothes. It is one that is cultivated with the help of others with whom one can be honest and who can give honest feedback—family, friends, colleagues, and parishioners. And it is nourished through personal spiritual discipline.

A second and somewhat different aspect of style, important in a time of limited mobility, is the capacity to be entrepreneurial. It is the willingness to be bold, energetic, innovative, and creative in one's pastoral leadership. An entrepreneurial style may conjure up the image of a brash, high pressure, obnoxious style, not unlike that of the proverbial used-car salesman. That is not what we mean. An individual with a low-keyed personality can have an entrepreneurial style in that she or he is self-motivating, has the capacity to take initiative and to see things through to their finish. The reasons for this should be obvious. The pastor who enables the development of creative, exciting programs that attract persons and help them grow in their faith will build not only a stronger congregation but also a stronger base for her or his ministry in that congregation.

The pastor who wants to serve a large congregation may have to build it rather than count on the denomination to arrange a move to such a church. This means that ministers will be left more to their own resources in developing their careers and can depend less on the institution to provide for them. Most churches have a substantial number of nonparticipants in their communities. Clergy who are skilled in evangelism will be the ones who will most likely increase their congregations and their bases of support. Of course, churches in sparsely populated areas have limited growth potential. The pastors of such congregations may find their satisfaction in the quality of their ministry and in areas of community service.

Our research clearly indicates that the effective minister is very much in demand. This is the one who provides strong leadership, makes things happen, is somewhat of an entrepreneur. In the current job market the more passive person who waits for the people to take the lead stands a good chance of being passed over. To survive in the present situation the clergyperson must assess his or her style of ministry to be certain that it is appropriate and effective.

PLAN A MOVE WITH CARE

In spite of limits to clergy mobility there are times in a minister's career when he or she should actively seek a change to another parish or church position. The clergyperson who can make such a decision freely, rather than under duress, is obviously in a stronger position; nevertheless, both situations occur and careful planning is essential in either case. A number of books deal in detail with strategies of job search[4]; therefore, we will be brief. There are several points we wish to emphasize that are appropriate in denominations where clergy are called and that are at least partly adaptable to appointive systems.

First of all, the clergyperson should follow the Socratic maxim: "Know thyself." He or she should not consider a move without clear self-knowledge of personal and professional strengths and limitations. An attempt should be made to state clearly one's career goals. Such knowledge enables the person to match herself or himself with the opportunities and expectations of potential jobs. Assistance in gaining self-knowledge and developing career goals is available in various career counseling programs.

Second, give considerable attention to preparing one's résumé. Writing a résumé or personal profile is an art about which much has been written. Nevertheless, we want to stress the importance of this step. While many denominations now have standardized forms for clergy profiles, completing such a profile to communicate effectively about oneself requires considerable skill. We were shown two clergy profiles using the same form and written by the same person. One was unimpressive and the other, written after some coaching, was extremely effectual in presenting the pastor to a search committee. The pastor did not change, but his profile did, and it gave him a much better chance of being invited for an interview.

Third, it is important to use both formal and informal channels for getting one's name before potential employers. Most studies of successful job searches for clergy and nonclergy stress the value of the informal system—the "old boy" network of friends and acquaintances. As we noted earlier, the informal system has not yet developed sufficiently for women; formal systems have proved more effective. Both should be utilized, preferably in combination. The formal system, especially a computerized system, gets one's name before a variety of potential employers in a way that would be impossible through informal channels. But a word to a prospective employer from a respected mutual friend or a judicatory executive is particularly effective.

Fourth, when one is invited for an interview or is exploring a possible new appointment in consultation with one's bishop, it is essential to find out in some detail what the parish or other job is really like, and what the expectations are. In a tight job market it is tempting to jump at the first job offered. This can be a disaster when there is incommensurability between one's own strengths and career goals, and the needs and expectations of the potential parish. The latter should be explored as carefully as one's own self-assessment. It may be painful to say no to a call or appointment when a person is desperate to move; however, desperation alone is rarely a basis for satisfactory decisions.

Perhaps the most important strategy of all for the clergy contemplating a change of position is to keep the initiative in his or her own hands. John C. Harris, who has had considerable experience in issues of clergy deployment within The Episcopal Church, advises that "the pastor must act as if he were without human resources of any kind in this world except those he identifies and organizes on his own behalf. That's obviously not true, of course, but he must learn to act as though it were true."[5] When one takes this stance, one moves from the passive dependency that many clergy deployment systems have fostered, to a proactive stance in one's own behalf. It does not guarantee a successful job change, but it increases the likelihood.

KNOW THE DENOMINATIONAL PLACEMENT SYSTEM

Ministers, unlike persons in some other professions, are only certified (ordained) to be employed in one denomination. While occasionally a minister will transfer from one denomination to another, the process can be difficult and at times virtually impossible. For the vast majority of clergy, this means, once a commitment has been made to a denomination and ordination achieved, that the options for employment are restricted to that denomination. It is imperative that the minister seeking employment or wishing to make a change know how the placement system in her or his denomination actually works.

120

In denominations that use an open method of deploying clergy (Baptist bodies, Church of God, Disciples of Christ, and United Church of Christ), the individual is, to a large degree, on his or her own. The denomination may publish a list of openings so that a pastor may know which congregations have vacancies. Some of these denominations maintain central offices where all clergy dossiers are kept on file. Also, some regional judicatories have staff persons assigned either full or part time to personnel functions. Their task includes helping pastors find churches and congregations locate pastors. Nevertheless, the minister must take the initiative in using these resources.

Denominations that employ a restricted open method of clergy deployment (Presbyterian bodies, The Episcopal Church, Lutheran groups, Reformed Church in America, and Church of the Nazarene) provide the individual with a greater degree of assistance in securing employment than do those with an open method. This may include assisting and sometimes requiring the congregation to do a self-study to determine its needs and goals, and the type of pastor most appropriate to the situation. The denomination may then allow the congregation to consider only persons who will meet their identified needs. Denominational officials on both the regional and national level are assigned to match up pastors and churches. While the decision as to which pastor is called is made by the congregation, denominational officials may play a significant advisory role to both the pastor and the local church.

Several denominations, including some with open or restricted open methods of deployment, maintain clergy dossiers in central files, some of which are computerized. Thus a pastor seeking a move can more easily have his or her dossier made available to vacant congregations throughout the denomination. The deployment agency may also have similar files for churches seeking a pastor or staff members. The central file, especially when computerized, readily identifies specific groups of persons (women, blacks, and so forth) or those with special skills (speaks Spanish, plays the organ) and matches them to the needs identified by churches. It is not apparent, however, that the computerized file will replace the informal network by which average ministers locate positions through personal contacts. Both are helpful.

121

Some theological seminaries related to denominations with open or restricted open clergy deployment methods maintain offices that seek to place their graduating students. Some also provide such services to their alumni seeking to relocate. These offices serve a brokering function of putting applicants and churches in touch with each other.

In what we have called a closed method of deployment (The United Methodist Church) the appointment of pastors is made by the bishop who presides over a regional judicatory (annual conference). The bishop is advised by district superintendents, who serve as liaison between the local churches and the pastors. Thus United Methodist pastors are assigned to local churches by the bishop, with varying degrees of consultation with the congregation and the individual minister.

Whatever the method of deployment, the minister seeking a different church needs to study carefully his or her denomination in order to understand how clergy are placed and how to maximize the chances for securing a suitable position. This can be done by seeking answers to several questions:

1. *At this time, in which part of the country are there the greatest number of openings?* Within the same denomination, availability of openings may vary regionally. Persons without experience who are seeking their first pastorate will generally fare better if they are willing to locate in areas of high demand for clergy.

2. *What are the official channels by which applicants can come to the attention of congregations with openings?* These would include the use of computerized clergy dossiers and the published list of churches seeking clergy. While a minister seeking a move should not rely solely on official channels, she or he should not ignore them.

3. *What other institutional channels are available to put me in contact with a church seeking a pastor?* These would include the placement offices of those theological seminaries providing such services to their graduates. Often a congregation that has had a positive experience with a pastor from a particular seminary will contact that seminary, hoping to find a new pastor with an orientation or style similar to the previous pastor's.

4. *Who are the persons most likely to know about openings and to*

be influential in determining who will be considered? These would include regional judicatory officials, such as district superintendents, synod president, association staff, and conference ministers. Such persons may influence which candidate a church seriously considers and even calls.

5. What persons in the informal denominational network can put me in touch with the churches seeking a pastor? The "old boy" system is alive and well in Protestant denominations. The person who is seeking a position has a greater opportunity for success if he or she is known throughout the system and can be recommended by colleagues whose opinions are respected by local church leaders. Such a system exists in any social institution, and the individual will ignore it at his or her peril.

While all the denominations have some similarities in their deployment methods, there are certain distinct differences. The person who is ordained in a particular denomination needs to study carefully the method by which clergy and churches are brought together, so that he or she will have the maximum opportunity of being considered for the positions most desired.

In the final analysis it must be noted that there is an element of chance in the process. A particular individual is in the right place at the right time. A church comes open the year a seminarian graduates. A friend at a denominational meeting mentions a person to the chairperson of a call committee. A bishop appoints a particular pastor to a church for reasons known only to the bishop. The factor in these instances may be considered chance, although some would give the Holy Spirit the credit (if the results are perceived as positive) or the denominational official the blame (if the results are seen as negative).

KNOW WHEN TO LEAVE THE MINISTRY

The ministry has traditionally been a hard profession to leave. A schoolteacher, a social worker, or a business person can change professions without anyone taking notice. If a pastor decides to leave the employment of the church and enter a secular profession, people will raise questions as to whether he has lost his faith or has been involved in some type of immoral conduct. Additionally, the concept of the call of God and a belief in an indelible ordination may leave former clergy with an extreme sense of guilt. As suggested in chapter 7, the idea of a lifetime ordination to the professional ministry (whether defined as indelible or not) needs to be reexamined. It may not be appropriate for an individual to spend his or her entire life as an ordained minister. The pastor who decides to change careers should be free to do so without being regarded as a moral failure or having to feel guilty for his or her action. The former pastor should be able not only to be part of the Christian community, but to continue involvement in the church as a volunteer.

The pressures on the clergy because of the oversupply will probably result in more persons with seminary training seeking secular employment. Some of these will feel that their financial needs cannot be met by the type of church positions they are able to secure. Others will find their upward mobility blocked and will decide to leave the church for other professions, ones that offer the kind of advancement they desire. Others will find the work of the pastor not what they had anticipated and will be unhappy with their choice of careers. Still others will simply lack the skills necessary for an effective ministry. For whatever reason, an individual should be able to leave the ministry without the stigma of being a moral failure. No one should remain if he or she is convinced that the ministry is not the right career. The person who continues in the ministry because of guilt or inertia will be neither effective nor happy.

It should be clear that a decision to leave the ministry is not to be taken lightly. The average pastor has invested a great deal of time and money in college and seminary training. Likewise, Protestant denominations highly subsidize theological education, so that they too have a substantial investment in each seminary graduate. However, a Master of Divinity degree is a professional degree leading to a career in some form of ministry. This degree does not prepare one for employment outside the church. As some persons who have decided to leave the ministry have discovered, to their surprise, the Master of Divinity degree is not a marketable item when looking for a nonchurch position.

Nevertheless, when an individual decides to leave the ministry, the church should attempt to assist in every appropriate way possible and help the person continue as a participant in the Christian community. An important source of help for clergy struggling with questions of staying or leaving are the various career counseling centers that have been developed in various regions. Many judicatories have financial aid available to assist clergy in using the services of these centers. Additionally, as previously noted, several denominations are developing other programs to support clergy who have decided to leave the ordained ministry.

While the current job market for clergy will be both painful and frustrating for many, it can also be a time for growth and renewal. To sum up, meeting the situation constructively involves understanding the factors that have created the current situation, using the occasion to reexamine one's call to the ministry, evaluating one's criteria of success, achieving a renewed sense of calling, assessing one's style of ministry, planning a move with care, knowing one's denominational placement system, and facing squarely the question of leaving or staying in the ordained ministry.

Chapter 9

Cassocks and Coveralls

The earliest pattern of support for Christian ministry was that of self-support. To be supported in a full-time ministry by the voluntary contributions of a congregation—the norm in most denominations today—was not the pattern in the early years of the church, nor did it become so until the third century A.D. Today clergy still combine cassocks with coveralls in various forms of total or partially self-supporting ministries (called "tentmaking" ministries after Paul's support of himself as a tentmaker). In this chapter we look at various forms of tentmaking ministries as important options for clergy and churches, especially in a changing and uncertain job market. We consider the strengths and the liabilities of such ministries, as well as strategies important for clergy and the churches if tentmaking options are to be pursued. Before addressing these issues, however, we take a brief look at the scope and types of tentmaking options.

SCOPE AND TYPES OF TENTMAKING MINISTRIES

A tentmaker clergy has been defined as "an active, ordained clergyperson in good standing who combines a church position or assignment with earning a major part of his/her compensation from sources outside the church."[1]

A 1974 survey of clergy in nineteen Protestant denominations revealed that 22 percent of the clergy in these denominations supplemented their income as clergy with some form of secular employment. This represented an increase of four percentage points since 1968 and seven percentage points since 1964. Thirteen percent of all clergy in 1974 worked more than twenty hours per week in their secular jobs. As might be expected, the lower the median salary paid in a denomination, the greater the number of clergy who worked more than twenty hours per week.[2] Nevertheless, regardless of median salary, in most denominations there is a sizable number of tentmakers working varying amounts of time in secular jobs.

Among the denominations we surveyed The Episcopal Church—with one of the highest median salaries—has had the most dramatic increase in the number of "nonstipendiary," or tentmaking, clergy. The number (including priests and perpetual deacons) grew from 602 in 1966 to 2,449 in 1974, an increase of 307 percent. In 1974 this group constituted 19 percent of all Episcopal clergy.[3]

If The Episcopal Church has experienced the most dramatic recent increase in tentmakers, the Southern Baptist Convention has the largest number of persons in this category. Called bivocationals, there were approximately 9,415 functioning in this capacity in 1976. This number constitutes approximately 30 percent of the total number of Southern Baptist clergy serving parishes. Of the total number of bivocationals, 7,323 (78 percent) were serving in small rural churches.[4] There are estimates that the percentage of bivocational Southern Baptist pastors will increase to 50 percent by the late 1980s.

Two of the denominations in our study—the Lutheran Church in America and The United Methodist Church—currently have restrictions against allowing ordained clergy to serve in tentmaking capacities, although there are attempts in each to have these restrictions changed. The United Methodist Church does have approximately 4,500 Local Pastors, unordained lay preachers who typically serve part time and are authorized to preach and perform sacramental functions on a limited basis. But such persons, who are essentially paraprofessionals, can only remain in this status for eight years, after which they must fulfill requirements for full-time, ordained status or be discontinued.

These examples suggest that there are various types or patterns of tentmaking ministries. One way of classifying such ministries is by the amount of time the clergyperson spends in secular-versus-church employment. In the 1974 survey mentioned above, Robert Bonn designated those clergy (9 percent of the total) working twenty or less hours per week in secular employment as moonlighters, and those working more than twenty hours (13 percent of the total) as part-time clergy.[5] It might be added that some tentmakers combine two church jobs rather than a church job and a secular job. For example, a clergyperson may work part time in a local church and part time for her or his denominational judicatory.

Another way of classifying those in tentmaking ministries is by the path taken into such a ministry. Some begin in a secular occupation and move part time into a pastorate. This has been the typical pattern for most of the Southern Baptist bivocational clergy and for United Methodist Local Pastors, who choose to fulfill the requirements for ordination. It has been estimated that approximately one third of the Episcopal candidates for the priesthood also follow this path, although not all of these remain as tentmakers.[6]

The other path into tentmaking is from ordained, full-time ministry into some degree of self-support in a secular job. Presumably, many moonlighters fall into this category. Additionally, there are ordained clergy who work considerably more hours per week in their secular employment than can be classified as moonlighting. In a period of an oversupplied job market for clergy we can expect this path into tentmaking to be taken by a growing number of ordained clergy. We suspect that the large increase in tentmakers in The Episcopal Church reflects this.

Another way of classifying tentmakers—particularly important from the perspective of the local church—is whether the clergy's work in the church is seen as providing a full (not necessarily full-time) ministry, or as providing a limited number of specific, contracted pastoral services, such as celebrating the sacraments and preaching. It makes a considerable difference to a congregation which pattern is followed. In the latter instance there is less likelihood that deep pastoral relationships will develop, nor is the clergyperson responsible for assisting in the development of the congregation's ministry and mission. In the former case, however, there is more possibility for mutuality, including mutual accountability, to develop, even when the clergyperson is not full time. The case of Richard, in chapter 1, is an illustration of how this may occur.

Two other variants of tentmaking ministries may be noted, but they are not our primary concern here. One is the worker-priest type. This is a person, typically fully ordained, who sees his or her vocation to ministry fulfilled in a secular job. The secular job, not the church, is the vehicle for the person's ministry. The other type of tentmaker is the layperson, "raised up" or identified from within a local congregation, who is trained and commissioned to carry out specified pastoral functions within the congregation. This pattern is an important one and is finding increasing use in small, isolated churches and in areas where clergy are in short supply.

This review of types of tentmaking clergy points out the diversity that exists in the way such ministries are developed and structured. Excluding the last two types mentioned (worker-priests and lay ministers), there are moonlighters and part-timers; there are those who come to ordination from a secular job and those who take the opposite path; and there are those for whom ministry in the church setting is a full (but not full-time) ministry, contrasted with those for whom it is a limited provision of specific pastoral services. These three ways of classifying tentmakers obviously cross-cut one another, making for an even greater diversity than we have suggested. The importance of the types is not their exhaustiveness, but their ability to suggest the range of possibilities open. Also, some patterns seem to have more promise and fewer liabilities than others.

WHY TENTMAKING?

Tentmaking patterns of ministry have been practiced for centuries; however, in recent years they seem to have come back into serious consideration, especially in denominations that have been heavily oriented toward full-time clergy as the normative pattern. Why this apparent shift?

From the standpoint of denominations and local churches, the reasons often boil down to financial ones—at least for the initial move to call or appoint a tentmaking clergyperson. When a congregation has too few members to support a full clergy salary, there are typically three options open to it, short of closing the church or merging it with another. It can appeal for a denominational subsidy to support a salary for a full-time pastor; it can join or yoke itself with one or more other small churches and share one or more clergy; or it can call or request a tentmaking clergyperson of one of the various types described above.

There are strengths and weaknesses in each of these options. Denominational subsidies make sense when there is the likelihood that the congregation can become self-supporting in a reasonable time; otherwise, subsidies foster an unhealthy dependency on the congregation's part. Also, denominations are finding it increasingly difficult to provide subsidies of any kind, as inflation brings about a shrinking financial base.

Various patterns of yoking of small churches to share one or more clergy have often worked well where clear contracts have been agreed upon between congregations sharing clergy, and between the clergy and the congregations. Such strategies, however, bring the complaint from congregations that their relationship with their pastor is diminished. He or she is not fully "theirs," a complaint that is also often made against some forms of tentmaking. While this may reflect the congregation's desire to control their pastor—which a one-to-one relation might make more possible—it may rather reflect a sense of loss of intimacy through having to share their "shepherd" with another "flock." A different sort of problem with yoking strategies for the denomination and for clergy is that they are strategies for a time of clergy shortage. When there are too many clergy, yoking further exacerbates the oversupply.

Thus tentmaking—the third option—becomes yet another way of addressing the needs of a congregation unable to afford a full-time clergyperson. It is not without its liabilities, but it seems to be growing in acceptance as an option for some congregations and denominations.

It is an option deliberately chosen by some clergy. In Bonn's comparison of moonlighting and part-time clergy, the primary reason given by both types of clergy was financial. They worked in secular jobs to augment their family income; however, this was considerably more important a reason for part-time clergy as compared with moonlighters. Approximately one fourth of the moonlighters indicated that they worked in secular jobs to obtain additional challenges or interests as compared with only 4 percent of the part-time clergy.[7] The need for additional challenge was also expressed in interviews we conducted with several tentmaker clergy who were participants in a pilot program (described below) to develop tentmaking or dual-role clergy. We found these tentmakers to be independent, highly motivated, and disciplined in their use of time—qualities that made it possible for them to combine other interests with a clergy position. Additionally, there is a small but growing number of clergy—including quite a few seminarians whom we interviewed—who have an interest in ministry in a small church, whether rural or urban. Given the financial realities of many small churches, such preferences often necessitate tentmaking if they are to be realized. Furthermore, tentmaking allows clergy in such financially marginal congregations to avoid resentment from parishioners who might otherwise be using as much as 90 percent of their parish finances to support a full-time pastor.

While small congregations, and clergy who wish to serve them are typically those who opt for a tentmaking ministry, there are some larger churches that have used tentmaking patterns for staff positions. And some churches have developed an entire multiple staff of tentmakers, who share the funds available for pastoral support and provide specialized leadership as part of a clergy team. This has met both the church's needs for ordained leadership and the interest of the clergy to pursue a specialized ministry.

Thus, for a variety of reasons, tentmaking is becoming more widely accepted in some denominations where full-time ordained ministry has been (and remains) the norm. It is not so positively viewed, however, in some denominations that have had a long history of part-time pastors or bivocationals. For example, several Southern Baptist and United Methodist denominational and seminary officials have expressed a desire to reduce reliance on such forms of ministry, which they viewed as second class in training and in competence. In most cases this negativity was reserved for tentmakers who came into the ministry part time from a secular job. There was less negativity to seminary-educated tentmakers.

IS TENTMAKING A VIABLE OPTION?

Despite criticisms we find tentmaking to be growing in acceptance, and it is increasingly being recommended to seminary students as an option for ministry in a tight job market and for those committed to ministry in small churches. In a 1977 survey of career plans of seminarians we found that 25 percent of the approximately

131

1,200 first- and third-year students responding (including 36 percent of the women) believed it very likely that they would be tentmakers.[8] Yet the question remains as to the viability of tentmaking as an option for ministry. What are its liabilities? Can they be overcome or minimized?

We look first at some liabilities of tentmaking that exist for clergy and their families, for churches, and for the judicatories. Then we describe a pilot program that has attempted to minimize these liabilities and develop a viable pattern of tentmaking ministry.

For clergy and their families, one liability centers around occupational status or prestige. Traditionally, clergy have had relatively high occupational status. The clergyperson was the "parson"—*the* person—in the community. While this has changed somewhat over the years, clergy have continued to be held in high esteem. However, some clergy who have moved from full-time to tentmaking ministry have felt that their occupational status has been lowered or demeaned. As an Episcopal clergyman who had tried tentmaking and then returned to full time expressed it, "No other profession expects its people to go out and earn money elsewhere in order to survive. . . . Some of us feel if you have something part time, it's not as good."[9] Such a feeling may be further exacerbated when the secular job is one of lower prestige than the clergy position. Also, tentmaking clergy may experience loss of status in the eyes of fellow clergy who view them as having failed to "make it" full time or as having "left the ministry."

Some loss of denominational status may be another liability for tentmakers. Denominational meetings of clergy are typically held at times that make it inconvenient or impossible for secularly employed clergy to attend. This may not only exclude them from attendance; it may also exclude them from the psychic rewards and recognition that come from functioning in leadership positions within the judicatory. There have been instances of loss of vote and of pension and insurance benefits by tentmaking clergy.[10]

Time demands of holding two jobs, even if both are part time, creates problems for some tentmaking clergy and their families. As one person put it, "Unless the minister-worker is single (an option I rejected) or is married to a spouse who wants to be 'assistant-to-minister' (an option my wife rejected), there seems to be insufficient time and energy to give one's best to two jobs and share life intimately with another person."[11] This is a common complaint of persons who have tried tentmaking. To minimize the problem requires not only a very self-disciplined person, but also a clear contract with the lay members of one's congregation. Additionally, it requires a secular job with relatively fixed time boundaries. A secular job that "never ends" (that is, one that does not have a limited weekly time demand) is likely to create severe conflicts for the tentmaking clergy.

A final liability of tentmaking for clergy—and for the judicatory as well—is that it complicates mobility. Not one, but two jobs must be taken into account. If the secular job is primarily a moonlighting phenomenon to supplement income, then there may not be a problem. But if the secular employment is more nearly a full-time occupation, there may be a conflict of priorities. Such a conflict is especially a problem for denominations like The United Methodist Church, with its appointive system for deploying clergy. The system depends on the availabiliy of the clergy to move on demand. If a person is strongly attracted to the secular job, and if it cannot be pursued in the new assignment, then a choice must be made about remaining a part of an itinerant ministry. This difficulty is not encountered as sharply in call systems of clergy deployment, but strong attachment to one's secular job may limit the range (in distance) within which one will consider a call from a new parish. At the very least it may create a conflict over job priorities.

There are also liabilities for congregations who opt for a tentmaking clergyperson. One of the first responses most congregations make when they move from full-time to one of the various tentmaking patterns is a sense of failure: "We are no longer able to support a full-time pastor; therefore, we are a failure as a church." The full-time pattern is so deeply engrained in our image of what should be that even to contemplate a different pattern meets resistance. A congregation may spend three fourths or more of its budget to support a full-time pastor rather than consider a less costly alternative. We do not support this view that a move to tentmaking (or yoking and other such strategies) is a mark of failure; nevertheless, it is common reaction that, where present, must be faced and worked through before tentmaking can be successfully adopted.

Another problem sometimes faced by a congregation with a tentmaker arises when the clergy's secular job is viewed as being "beneath the dignity" of the status attributed to the ordained ministry. "Would you want your pastor to be your plumber?" This is the kind of complaint made by laity who experience a discrepancy between the status they attribute to the role of the clergy and that of their tentmaking pastor's secular job if it is perceived to be of distinctly lower status. (We have nothing against plumbers. We simply illustrate the kind of status discrepancy that is sometimes experienced.) These two liabilities for congregations considering tentmaking are basically perceptual. They exist in the way that the tentmaking situation is defined. This does not diminish their importance, since situations defined as real are often real in their consequences. Such perceptions and definitions can be overcome so that their negative consequences are reduced or eliminated.

A third liability for congregations results, not from perceptions, but from the demands that a tentmaking pattern of ministry may make on laity in the congregation. If the ministry of the church is to be more than a "holding pattern," laity will have to assume considerably greater responsibility for the church's ministry than many are accustomed to do. A part-time clergyperson can be secured to hold services and do pastoral visitation to the sick and shut-in, with the result that little is demanded of laity. However, if this is the only ministry that is taking place, most congregations will suffer. Successful use of a tentmaking pastor requires significant involvement by laity in ministry.

A third part of the church system for which tentmaking holds some liabilities is the judicatory. Perhaps the most serious problem judicatories have with tentmaking patterns is that of mobility. As previously noted, tentmaking can require a complex juggling act to coordinate the call or appointment of a tentmaking minister to a congregation and the clergy's secular employment. This difficulty alone has dissuaded some judicatory officials from enthusiasm about tentmaking.

A further factor that may dampen judicatory enthusiasm is the perception of some loss of control over the tentmaking clergyperson by the denomination. Secularly employed clergy are often viewed as less dependent on the church (both congregation and denomination) than full-time clergy. At worst, this may foster negativity toward tentmaking by judicatory officials who can no longer keep tentmakers "barefoot and pregnant," in the ecclesiastical sense. More charitably (and perhaps more accurately), some negativity results from the fact that tentmakers do not always have time, nor do their schedules permit them, to become as significantly involved in denominational affairs as their full-time counterparts. The denomination has less claim, therefore, on their time and energy.

Such liabilities of tentmaking for clergy and their families, for congregations, and for judicatories may discourage some from considering tentmaking as a viable option. We concur that it is not a viable option for all clergy or congregations. The costs will be too great for some to pay. But for those willing to face these costs realistically, tentmaking can be a significant form of ministry. How can the costs be reduced and the liabilities we have listed be avoided or minimized? An interesting and important pilot project has recently sought to answer these questions.

THE CLERGY OCCUPATIONAL DEVELOPMENT AND EMPLOYMENT PROJECT

The Clergy Occupational Development and Employment Project (CODE) was a pilot project that had as its primary purpose developing a model for assisting clergy to become tentmakers (defined as dual-role clergy) in a way that would be seen as a legitimate form of ministry by themselves, by congregations, and by denominations. Made possible by a grant from the Lilly Endowment, Inc., CODE published a report of findings and experiences, including a manual for those interested in developing a dual-role ministry.[12] Space does not permit a detailed summary of the project; however, a brief description and report of several of the major learnings will indicate how CODE sought to develop a positive approach to tentmaking and to overcome some of its liabilities.

A clear definition of dual-role, or tentmaking, ministry was early adopted by the CODE management committee, consisting of representatives of the American Baptist Churches, The United Presbyterian Church in the U.S.A., and United Church of Christ denominations in western New York State. Dual-role ministry involves the following characteristics:

1. It refers to an ordained, fully trained clergyperson who has previous experience (usually ten to fifteen years minimum) as a full-time professional minister.
2. The clergyperson works full time in a secular occupation (forty hours per week).
3. The clergyperson works approximately twenty to twenty-four hours per week either in a specialized staff function or as sole clergy in a partnership ministry with laity that is defined as a *full* although *not full-time* ministry.
4. The clergyperson is compensated by the congregation for his or her services.

Clearly, the CODE dual-role model is not what we referred to earlier as moonlighting; nor is it a true nonstipendiary model, where the clergy volunteers services to the congregation; nor is it a "holding operation," by which a congregation contracts for a limited number of services; nor is it a model for lay paraprofessional ministries.

Functioning with this definition, the process developed by CODE approaches tentmaking from a systems perspective. That is, there is recognition that several fronts have to be attacked together to overcome some of the liabilities of tentmaking ministry. These fronts include the interested clergy, the judicatories, potential employing congregations, and secular employers.

For clergy, there are at least two basic steps once a decision has been made to explore a dual-role ministry. First, there is a professional assessment by a trained personnel specialist (in CODE's case, an industrial psychologist). The assessment considers such things as motivation for seeking dual-role status, ability to separate roles, flexibility, organization, and skills. Second, clergy are provided counseling by a panel of business leaders and personnel managers in further assessing skills, developing competence in the search for a secular job, writing résumés, and setting realistic objectives for both ministry and secular jobs. Once these two steps are completed and judicatory approval is granted, the job search begins for both a church and a secular job.

Judicatory officials are a second key aspect to CODE's approach. They are essential in providing legitimation for dual-role ministries and for being channels of communication between clergy interested in dual-role and churches willing to consider dual-role clergy for senior pastor or staff positions. Without the judicatories' stamp of approval on dual-role ministries and their efforts to bring interested clergy and churches together, there is little likelihood of success. Furthermore, judicatory leaders play an important role in helping churches and clergy to negotiate contracts and in providing ongoing support for dual-role clergy.

Likewise, congregations have to be prepared for the move to a dual-role pastor or staff person. CODE advocates a self-study by the congregation, with judicatory assistance, including an assessment of pastoral needs. Implications of moving to a dual-role ministry are fully explored, and a commitment is sought from the congregation to pursue dual-role. As the congregation begins its search for a dual-role minister, it also provides some assistance to the prospective clergy in the search for secular employment by suggesting potential employers and seeking to arrange interviews. A further key element in the congregation's role is that of accepting the implications of the dual-role pattern for the ministry of the laity. There must be a commitment to shared ministry, including developing training necessary for laity to assume their role as partners in ministry. When this commitment is made, congregation and clergy are helped to work out the practical implications of the commitment by writing mutual job descriptions and expectations.

As a final step in the systems approach, CODE works with area employers to encourage acceptance of dual-role clergy as potential employees. Employers need to understand that the job-seekers are active ministers who intend to continue to function as clergy and are not ministerial dropouts. Because they want to continue to function actively as clergy, job-seekers are often content to seek entry level jobs, with more limited responsibilities than their education and experience might dictate. Potential employers need to understand this situation. Finally, employers sometimes need reassurance that the clergyperson is not planning to use the secular job as a platform from which to evangelize fellow workers.

Using this multifaceted approach to tentmaking, CODE worked

with some sixty clergy during its two and a half years. A majority of these clergy decided that dual-role, as defined by CODE, was demanding in ways not suitable for them. Some dropped out without completing the process. Several reaffirmed their commitment to a single-role ministry, and a small number used the process to assist them in deciding to leave the ministry. Five persons completed the entire CODE process and became dual-role clergy.

While five dual-role clergy out of sixty who began the process may be viewed by some as a small accomplishment, CODE's contribution goes considerably beyond its quantitative achievements. As a pilot project, CODE has provided a careful and systematic approach to tentmaking that can be adapted and modified by various denominations to meet their particular needs. It is a model that overcomes a number of the liabilities that were previously noted. Although tentmaking will probably remain an option for a limited number of clergy and congregations, those that do pursue it will benefit greatly from the CODE experience. It is an option that will be considered increasingly in this period of oversupply.

Chapter 10

The Church System and Clergy Employment

The judicatory official frowned as he said, "I think my job is getting more difficult. George has done a good job at St. Paul's, but he needs to move. I simply have not been able to find another church for him. Maybe we have been ordaining too many people."

The denominations, and particularly the regional judicatories, are one part of the church system that is being affected by the oversupply of ministers. A second part of the system influenced by the present job market is the local congregation; theological seminaries are the third. This chapter examines ways in which these three elements might respond to the current oversupply of clergy that are to the mutual benefit of all concerned. We begin with the local church.

THE LOCAL CHURCH

The local church employs the vast majority of ordained Protestant clergy. An oversupply of clergy is a new experience for this generation of church members; they have been accustomed to a shortage. The oversupply affects them primarily at the time they have a vacancy or when they wish their present pastor to leave. There are several specific actions that could be of benefit to both the congregation and the pastor.

The Hiring Process

The current surplus does not make the selection of a pastor by a congregation any easier; it may actually make it more difficult.

Although call committee members may still approach their task worried about locating any effective clergy willing to come to their church, they often find themselves overwhelmed with such a large number of applicants that they have difficulty sorting out the significant differences among the persons seeking the position. One congregation that received dossiers of 150 potential clergy actually considered only the first seventy-five; the remainder were not even read.

There are a number of ways that congregations and their call committees can make the period during a change of pastors a productive one for congregational growth. The following suggestions do not exhaust all the steps in the vacancy process; rather, they are ones particularly pertinent to a period of clergy surplus.[1] (While the suggestions are primarily pertinent to congregations that call their clergy, some can be adapted helpfully for churches whose clergy are appointed.)

First, it is very important that the congregation seeking a new pastor have a clear sense of the nature and mission of that particular local church. The people need to know who they are as a congregation and what their priorities and goals are in order to secure the kind of pastor that will help them achieve these priorities. With an increasingly large number of clergy seeking positions, the congregation with a vacancy can search for the person who will be best for the church at this particular time in its history. One way to accomplish such self-understanding is through a congregational self-study, using one or more of a variety of processes that have been developed. Often judicatories provide assistance to congregations in doing such a study. Some judicatories require a study as part of a formal process of "vacancy counseling." It is important for the call committee to involve the entire congregation in the self-study process and in clarification of goals and priorities.

Obtaining a list of potential candidates is the next step. Both formal and informal channels should be used to secure names and dossiers; however, the congregation with a clear sense of its identity will be able to specify more accurately the type of person it wants and thus reduce the sheer volume of names it will receive. The formal system, especially when it has been computerized, can provide a broad range of candidates that may otherwise be overlooked in the informal networks. This provides an important resource both to committees and candidates. However, informal networks, especially recommendations of trusted judicatory leaders and friends who know the parish, continue to be a significant source of potential candidates.

Because a congregation will typically have a large number of candidates from which to select during this time of clergy surplus, the call committee needs to develop clear criteria for judging among candidates' dossiers. Time spent in sharing rationales for interest or lack of interest in particular candidates will be well spent. In such ways mutual understanding is developed among the committee members and criteria are sharpened that will be helpful when the interview process begins.

As a committee begins to narrow its list to those whom it will interview, it is useful to develop a list of questions to be addressed to interviewees. One judicatory in New England arranges for the committee to engage in a practice interview with a clergyperson who the executive feels would be appropriate for the church but who is not a candidate.

Technology may also be a boon to a committee that has more interesting candidates than it can afford to interview face to face. One committee rented speakerphones and conducted initial screening interviews with potential candidates by telephone.

As the committee conducts interviews, whether face to face or by telephone, it is important that it communicate its decision to the interviewee. If the committee members decide not to pursue a candidate further, they should inform him or her of their decision and indicate why they reached it. Failure to provide a rejected candidate with honest feedback as to why the decision was made is to do him or her an injustice.

Finally, because of the surplus of clergy, a committee may be tempted to secure a minister for the lowest salary possible. While it is a "buyer's market," such a strategy may be self-defeating in the long run and also will do a disservice to the prospective pastor and his or her family. Clergy salaries are already quite low, and the quality of the present and future ministry of the church will not be helped by congregations that attempt to get by for the lowest possible salaries.

Evaluating and Supporting the Pastor

The oversupply of clergy can mean that the congregation will have its minister for a longer period of time, not a shorter one. With the slowing down of mobility, pastors may remain in the same place longer simply because they have no place to which they can go. A result is that both the minister and the laity will have to work more closely together to see that the minister's work is appropriate for the church. As the local situation changes, the pastor may need to be helped to change his or her emphasis.

Lack of opportunities for the pastor to move will also mean that problems between pastor and people will have to be worked through; they will not be solved by the simple process of the minister going off and leaving them behind, possibly for his or her successor to handle. This is healthy, because it will force both pastor and church members to deal with issues that could be avoided almost indefinitely by having a succession of pastors who remained only a short time.

Evaluation of the work of the pastor must become more formal and systematic. At this point, work is just beginning in this area. It is essential that the pastor really know how well he or she is doing so that appropriate changes can be made. Laity need to develop the capacity to give honest and loving critique. Often formal evaluations of clergy are extremely positive and polite, while "corridor criticisms" are quite negative. There is no way the element of threat can be completely removed from any process of evaluation. The evaluators and, especially, those being evaluated make themselves vulnerable. Evaluation can be made universal, however, and thus an expected part of a pastor's career. There is still a long way to go in this area, but the effectiveness of the ministry of the church will make clergy evaluation essential.

Termination of Clergy

As has been pointed out, the oversupply of clergy may make it more difficult for the clergyperson to leave a congregation, even when it is in the best interest of both parties. A minister is reluctant to resign if he or she has no other church to which to go. Nevertheless, both clergy and call committees (or bishops) make mistakes. There are times when, for the good of all, the relationship of a minister and

142

a congregation must be terminated. This decision should not be reached lightly, but only after thorough study and prayerful consideration of all the factors involved.

The best way to avoid the necessity of termination is through careful hiring procedures. But when mistakes are made, it is essential that the church not retain a minister solely because she or he does not have another church position waiting. The laity in the congregation or in other congregations can assist the pastor to find other employment. This may be the best course for both the individual and for the congregation, however difficult and unpleasant it may seem at the time. More will be said below about assisting clergy to leave the ordained ministry.

THE REGIONAL JUDICATORIES

In dealing with the oversupply of clergy, the regional judicatories occupy a crucial position. There are several things these groups need to consider in regard to the ministerial job market.

The Need for Better Records

In our research we discovered that judicatories do not keep adequate statistical records that would help them predict their need for ordained clergy in the future. The national denominations collect a variety of statistical data, but here again much of this is either not useful or accessible in a form to help determine the need for ministers.

An example is data on the age of clergy. Most denominations have a policy regarding the age at which a minister must retire. Generally, there is an age at which retirement is optional and a later one when it is required. It would thus be possible to anticipate with some degree of accuracy the number of positions coming vacant through retirement. Yet, to our surprise, we found that complete or easily accessible age data was not available in a number of major denominations studied.

In addition to data on the age of clergy, information could be collected on the length of tenure in positions, ages at which persons enter the ministry, the dropout rate, data on availability of congregations that are or could be able to employ a pastor, and the trends in the deployment of ordained persons. Such data could help judicatories better predict their need for clergy in both the short and long term.

Support and Affirmation

The regional judicatory is the body charged with admitting, deploying, supporting, and assisting the termination of clergy. Additionally, the clergy who serve within the bounds of the regional judicatory make up the ministers' professional peer group. These are the persons who often provide colleague support and are the ones against whom the individual pastor evaluates his or her effectiveness and success. In a time of oversupply, the peers in the region are in a key position to provide the support and affirmation that every minister needs.

Also, in time of oversupply, promotion to a larger congregation may be less frequent; even moving to another church is increasingly difficult. Success must be seen in terms of performing an effective ministry, of witnessing and serving in the local parish, no matter what the prestige or the status of that particular church may be. To develop such an attitude will require clergy to consider again the source of the authority for their ministry, the biblical basis for the task to which they have been called. It will mean coming to grips with the high level of materialism that is prevalent in the church today. This can be a painful task, but it is one that is not only necessary, but can increase the effectiveness of the ministers and of the congregations they serve. Judicatory officials can play an important role in this process of clarification by the success criteria they communicate and through providing occasions for reflection on such criteria. Thus the pastor who serves two small rural congregations can be perceived as an effective minister (which he or she may be) and not have success tied solely to the institutional setting in which that ministry is performed.

The above deals with the general climate of opinion regarding the clergy. There are, in addition, some specific actions that judicatories (and/or the national denominations) can take. These include programs of continuing education, which can help ministers at certain crucial points in their careers, and services such as career assessment and counseling, either by the judicatory or by one of the independent organizations available for career assessment and counseling of clergy. These programs are designed to assist clergy to

144

reassess their careers, to determine their strengths and areas where they can improve, and to help them determine future directions. Judicatories and/or local churches that assist clergy to avail themselves of such programs usually find the cost of doing so a worthwhile expense.

In chapter 8 we noted that there are three critical points in the minister's career at which programs of continuing education and support can be invaluable: the first three to five years after seminary graduation; the midcareer transition; and preretirement. Since regional judicatory leaders are sufficiently close to clergy experiencing these career stages, they are especially alert to particular needs and special circumstances. They can aid the clergy during these periods by developing support and continuing education programs within the judicatory or by making it possible for clergy to participate in other existing programs.

Requirements for Ordination

A trend in most mainline denominations has been to increase the requirements for ordination. Four years of college and three of seminary are now the expected norm. The oversupply of clergy seems to be a factor in the decision by some judicatories to increase further the formal requirements for ordination as a way of controlling the quantity and quality of applicants. These are taking several forms, including a number of specific courses to be taken in seminary, a lengthening of the probationary period, and serving an internship in a local church. The assumption is that the increased requirements will produce better-trained pastors and will weed out those not willing to make the necessary sacrifices to qualify for the ordained ministry.

The pressure to increase the number of requirements and the length of preparation for ordination has tended to come from the clergy rather than the laypeople. It does not necessarily follow that lengthening the time spent in preparation increases the effectiveness of the minister—at least beyond a certain but unidentified point. The seven or eight years of preparation may tend to raise the candidate's expectations far beyond the level of the position that he or she is likely to attain. It is not uncommon or incorrect for the minister to compare the amount of training required for ordination to that required of the physician. The implication is that the clergy should be better compensated because of the amount of training they have had, that is, similar to the physician. This is not likely to occur, especially since the demands for more educational requirements have come from the ministers themselves.

A serious matter related to the increased requirements for ordination is the moral obligation that an institution has to an individual if it permits him or her to invest seven or eight years in preparation for a position that may or may not be available. If judicatories are going to increase requirements, they must give serious attention to preliminary screening of candidates, even before seminary where possible, and to making decisions regarding acceptance or rejection as early as feasible. They must also help prospective clergy to have a clear understanding of the kinds of positions likely to be available. The deployment agencies of both Presbyterian denominations are giving candidates a realistic picture of the job market. It is the only fair way to deal with persons who are expected to devote their lives to the church.

Care in Admission

The most crucial decisions judicatories make are those relating to candidates for the ministry. Here they decide not only the careers of the applicants for the next thirty-five or forty years, but who will lead the congregations for the same period. The surplus of ministers is putting the screening committees under great pressure. The present employment situation presents several dangers for these groups that we would like to highlight.

The first is a kind of ecclesiastical nepotism, whereby a judicatory will tend to give preference to candidates from its churches at the expense of the more qualified person from elsewhere in the denomination. This is a natural reaction in a period when jobs are scarce to take care of one's own. In addition to being basically unfair, such a practice is shortsighted, as it places emphasis on the wrong criteria when admitting persons into the ministry.

A second danger is for screening committees to back away from the hard decisions regarding candidates about whom there is doubt. This tends to avoid a clear-cut determination and passes the decision to the local church who must decide to call or not to call a certain pastor, or simply puts a less than adequate minister into the system.

146

One United Methodist official commented, "Our conference board of the ministry can't seem to say no to anyone who claims to have been called by God, no matter how inept that person may appear."

The third and greatest danger judicatories must avoid is to accept only "ecclesiastical organization men and women" who will not rock the boat, who will fit neatly into the present system. Any institution, and particularly the church, needs persons who will challenge the accepted policies and bring fresh, creative, and sometimes controversial ideas. In a time of a surplus of candidates the denomination that accepts only the "safe" candidates for the ministry does so at its own peril.

Advocacy for Women Clergy

Judicatories will need to continue to assume an advocacy position for ordained women in the period ahead. While women are securing pastoral positions in increasing numbers, there are still congregations that will not consider women. If women are going to be ordained and to secure positions in the church system, the persons responsible for clergy placement will have to make every effort to see that congregations have the opportunity to consider women for the available positions.

Placement officials in the judicatories will be in an unenviable position in the period immediately ahead. One woman church leader predicts that the feminist battle to make seminaries more receptive to women students is moving from the seminaries to the judicatories. Placement officials will be caught between the demands of the women for access to the opportunities for employment in the church system and the unwillingness of some congregations to employ women pastors. Furthermore, women, like minority persons, can assume that any rejection was due to sexism or racism, whether this was or was not the case. Thus the placement agencies will continue to receive criticism. However, this should not lessen their advocacy for securing employment opportunities for all qualified persons.

Outplacement

As we have noted, there are times when it is in the best interests of clergy and the denomination for a person to leave the ordained ministry. For a variety of reasons, some based on a belief in indelible ordination and others on the central place one's occupation has in shaping one's identity, a decision to leave the ordained ministry can be a traumatic experience. If the decision is involuntary, it can be devastating. One pastor, who was requested to take early retirement involuntarily, took his own life. There is need for just and loving means of helping clergy who are exiting the ordained ministry, voluntarily or involuntarily, to do so with dignity. Some denominations, especially The American Lutheran Church and the Lutheran Church in America, are in process of developing "outplacement" programs for clergy.

Outplacement, a process being used increasingly by business, involves making available various forms of support to enable persons to make successful transitions from one occupation to another. A Lutheran Church in America proposal includes (1) assisting clergy to find temporary employment while the person receives necessary counseling and training for a new occupational role; (2) economic assistance, where needed, to take care of moving expenses and debt liquidation; (3) career counseling to assist clergy in self-assessment and exploring options; (4) coaching in job seeking; and (5) assistance in needed remedial or specialized training. The proposal argues that such programs are not only means of serving exiting clergy and their families, but they also are in the self-interest of the denomination. They help to foster a continuing positive relation to the church of persons in which the church has invested up to $30,000 each in their education.[2]

THE THEOLOGICAL SEMINARIES

Of the components of the church system the theological seminaries have the least direct impact on the clergy job market. They recruit students and train them for the ministry; they do not make the decision as to who shall be ordained or employed. Schools of theology, however, are in a unique position to make a positive contribution to the clergy and the churches as they struggle with the oversupply of ministers.

A Realistic Picture of Ministry

The primary task of the seminary is to prepare its graduates for a career in the professional ministry, a large proportion of whom will be employed as pastors of local churches. Thus the educational program should have as one of its objectives giving students a realistic understanding of what life in the parish is like. This should include helping students understand the factors influencing the job market they will seek to enter at the conclusion of their training. Students also need to understand that most of the positions will be in the small-membership churches, and they should receive training appropriate to those churches.

Employment opportunities outside the church for persons with a Master of Divinity degree are relatively narrow. It is a professional degree with relatively little market value outside the areas of religion. It is essential that students understand this. This will require more interchange between school and the profession and will encourage seminaries to move farther beyond solely the graduate school model in their training of prospective clergy.

Dual Competency

The present job market will likely mean that more clergy will pursue dual careers or become tentmakers. If this is to be the case, more ordained persons will need to acquire the skills to make it possible. Schools of theology are not prepared to train persons for anything other than church-related positions. They can, however, encourage students who are so inclined to acquire an additional skill. Thus graduates would be better equipped to earn income outside the church. Seminaries can do this by cooperating with other educational institutions in the area on joint programs and by arranging their schedule to permit students to pursue training in areas other than religion. An important factor, if this is to happen, is the attitude of faculty, who in most cases are reluctant to relinquish some of their demands on the students in order to make acquiring a dual competency possible. They will have to be convinced that it is essential for the future ministry of their students. Additionally, realistic approaches to dual competency must be developed. Some occupations do not combine easily with ordained ministry, to allow persons to function in both roles. This seems to be the case for dual competency in ministry and in law. Time demands and other factors in the two professions have made such combinations relatively

149

unsuccessful. However, programs combining education for ministry with social work have had greater success.

Continuing Education

Seminaries have a responsibility and an opportunity in the area of continuing education for clergy. At present, most seminaries view continuing education as something to be done on the margins of faculty time. Often it has been a way of enabling faculty to supplement their salaries. Additionally, the prevailing purpose of continuing education has tended to be to provide alumni a chance to find out what has been going on in the various academic disciplines in the years since graduation. Such an approach to continuing education will not meet the needs of today's clergy.

Clergy who engage in continuing education are not at the same place as they were as Master of Divinity students. Continuing education must be relevant to the situation of ministry they are now experiencing. A shortened version of a recent M.Div. or Ph.D. course may be interesting, but it will not likely be adequate to the needs of local church pastors. Seminary faculty who are effective in meeting the continuing education needs of clergy are those who can help them reflect on their ministry experiences in light of the resources of the disciplines the faculty represent.

The current clergy surplus may also be an occasion for seminaries to move continuing education to a more central rather than marginal concern. This has already occurred for some seminaries that have developed in-career Doctor of Ministry programs. Seminaries that have made Ph.D. programs their other major degree focus are finding it increasingly difficult to place their graduates in teaching positions. The time, resources, and energy that some have invested in Ph.D. programs may be more appropriately spent in developing continuing education programs for clergy.

Other Roles for Seminaries

Bringing continuing education for clergy into the central focus of the seminary's task is one possible new role for seminaries in a time when there are pressures to restrict enrollments and to avoid training students for nonexistent jobs. In addition to continuing education, other new constituencies and roles for seminaries are possible.

Laity are an important potential new constituency for seminaries.

There is renewed concern and excitement over the mutual ministry of laity and clergy. As this develops, laity are asking for assistance in becoming more competent in the exercise of their ministries. This has two implications for seminaries. On the one hand, some laity will be candidates for programs designed to enable them to function in traditional pastoral roles in their congregations, especially in situations where congregations cannot afford full-time ordained leadership. On the other hand, there are many laity who want education that will equip them to fulfill their ministries in their roles in society. Here the education needed is that which provides opportunities for theological and ethical reflection on the day-to-day life situations that laity face. Meeting either or both of these needs is an option for seminaries that seek to discover new roles and constituencies.[3] An especially creative experience is possible when this is done with some interface between laity and clergy (or candidates for ordination) in the educational process. This can help to break down the clerical professionalism to which we referred in chapter 8.

In addition to becoming centers for continuing education for clergy and for laity, some seminaries may find new and important roles in research and experimentation on behalf of the church. Both basic and applied research are needed to serve the intellectual and the practical life of the church and to provide innovative models of ministry and mission that have been tested and carefully evaluated.

It is not easy for seminaries and other components of the church system to shift their focus to new roles or to serve new constituencies. There is, of course, a danger in precipitous responses to the pressures of the current employment situation for clergy. The temptation is to take irreversible actions that appear to solve the short-term problem but which may not be best over the long term. An equal danger is that the force of institutional inertia will prevent seminaries and other parts of the church system from using the present situation as an opportunity to question traditional assumptions and practices and to become more responsive to the present and emerging needs of the church. This twin danger is the subject of the Afterword.

Afterword

Caution and Optimism

We want to conclude this analysis of the job market for Protestant clergy on a dual note of caution and of optimism. The employment situation for ministers is going to continue to be tight in the period immediately ahead. It is not, however, a time to follow the example of Chicken Little and assume the sky is falling, or the ostrich who buried its head in the sand.

We have seen that a variety of factors affect clergy supply and demand. Some of these, such as the large number of young adults beginning their careers, are beyond the control of the church. Others, such as the effort put into increasing church membership, are the result of what the denominations do or fail to do. The future of the church, including job opportunities for ordained clergy, will depend both on the dominant factors in the larger society and on the ways in which the churches respond to these factors.

Predicting the future with any accuracy is hazardous, especially when the future will be determined by the interaction of a variety of complex forces such as those influencing the clergy job market. What is certain is that the future will in part be determined by the actions the denominations take to meet the present situation. A decision to limit drastically the number of persons entering the ministry could result in problems in the supply of clergy twenty or thirty years from now. The closing of a theological seminary would mean the irretrievable loss of a resource needed in the future. The point is not that drastic action is never appropriate, but that long-term trends and needs be carefully considered whenever action is taken. Any decision made to influence or change the church's ministry and mission is a calculated risk. Such decisions need to be based on careful theological reflection, on the best data available, and on a reading of the present and future needs of the church. Our word of caution is not to act precipitously, thereby creating a long-term problem by attempting to solve a crisis of the moment.

Yet we wish also to affirm that the present period of clergy oversupply provides the churches with an opportunity for creative change. The old structures are coming under increasing pressure, and the old ways of operating are being challenged. Every institution, including the churches, tends to want to retain the familiar ways of operating even after their effectiveness is in doubt. Forces in both the church and the society are making it impossible for the status quo to be maintained. Changes will certainly occur; the direction of these changes and the quality and effectiveness of the church's ministry and mission will depend on the insight and skill with which denominational leaders respond to these changes.

The danger is that church leaders will try to preserve the present ways of doing things, ways which were effective in the past. Generals are sometimes accused of preparing to fight the next war with the tactics of the past; they are not alone in their loyalty to a method long after it has outlived its effectiveness. The greatest danger for the church in this time of clergy oversupply is that it will "draw the wagons in a tight circle" and try to live only by the old rules governing the education, ordination, and deployment of clergy. As the church employment system feels itself under greater pressure, such rules may be interpreted with greater strictness.

The development of the Christian church has not been one of steady, upward progress. Periods of growth have been followed by times of falling away and decline. Revivals have not been predictable events. One cannot consider the history of the church, with its long succession of faithful and less than faithful followers, its defeats and victories, its tragedies and triumphs, without being optimistic about the future. The church is an institution that, to some degree, is unpredictable; no one can foretell the tasks to which God may call the church in the period ahead.

The present oversupply of clergy may seem to be shaking the very foundations of the professional ministry. Yet out of even this experience new meanings of ordination and new patterns of ministry and church life may be emerging. These can include new roles for the ordained clergy and greater involvement of laypersons in giving leadership to the local church.

For those who must make the decisions concerning the recruitment, training, and deployment of clergy in this time of oversupply, we give these words of advice. First, do your best to understand the situation and the factors that are influencing the clergy job market. Particularly, note the long-term trends and how today's decisions may have an impact on events a decade or two in the future.

Second, consider the present period to be one of opportunity. The present shaking of the foundations is giving the church a chance to reexamine the whole issue of ordination and the tasks of clergy and laity. While the process may be painful, the results can be beneficial and can result in a more effective ministry.

Third, face the future and its problems and opportunities with optimism. It can never be assumed that the present trends influencing the clergy job market will continue indefinitely. Factors as yet unknown may influence the need for clergy. The church has been one of society's most durable institutions. It has not only survived, but has flourished in a variety of social contexts. There is little reason to assume this will change.

In the final analysis the church is not called to be successful, but to be faithful. Its objective is not institutional growth or providing employment for the ordained clergy. Its objective is to witness to the gospel and to minister in the name of Jesus Christ. Whatever institutional problems arise, including the oversupply of clergy, must be seen and dealt with in the perspective of the basic tasks to which the church has been called.

In all this we have said nothing about the likely continuation of the religious ferment evident in the larger society. There are those who feel we are in the early stages of a religious awakening. The growth of the evangelical and the charismatic movements would lend evidence to this. If this were the case, the need for clergy, as indicated by the present trends, could be significantly altered. However, religious awakenings are impossible to predict. The Spirit, like the wind, blows where it wills, and we do not presume to forecast its direction.

154

Appendix

The tables and figures that follow are from an earlier report of the findings of our research (Carroll and Wilson, *The Clergy Job Market: Oversupply and/or Opportunity* (Hartford, Conn.: Hartford Seminary Foundation, 1978). They have been alluded to at appropriate places in the preceding pages and provide support for some of the analyses and inferences we have drawn. The tables in the Appendix begin with Table 3, since the first two tables are in the main body of the text.

Table 3 Percentage Changes for Various Indicators of Supply and Demand in Selected Denominations, 1955-65, 1965-75

	Inclusive Membership		Churches		Total Clergy[a]		Clergy Serving Churches[b]	
	55-65	65-75	55-65	65-75	55-65	65-75	55-65	65-75
American Baptist Churches	1.6	4.2	-6.6[d]	-1.2[d]	1.2[d]	3.9[d]	-15.6[d]	11.7[d]
Church of God (Anderson)	15.9	16.1	6.6	-2.0	0.1	7.4	1.5	0.1
Church of the Nazarene	26.9	28.4	12.0	3.3	19.4	16.6	2.5	na
Disciples of Christ	1.1	-32.4	1.6	-44.1	4.5	-14.5	-21.7[d]	25.5[d]
Episcopal Church	26.7	-16.7	4.0[c]	-4.6	36.1	18.2	na	-12.7[d]
Lutheran Church in America	13.8	-3.9	7.1	-1.7	26.8	10.2	22.8	-1.7
Presbyterian Church, U.S.	17.2	-8.6	4.0	0.4	26.5	21.5	15.7	2.7
Reformed Church in America	20.7	-7.9	15.3	-2.7	21.3	18.2	25.5	1.5
Southern Baptist Convention	27.2	18.2	11.3	3.3	26.8	57.1	24.5	2.2
United Church of Christ	2.2	-12.1	-16.1	-5.9	2.1	9.7	24.4	-24.6
United Methodist Church	9.8	-9.8	-2.8	-9.4	9.0	6.6	na	na
United Presbyterian Church, U.S.A.	20.9	-12.4	5.3	-4.7	29.1	8.1	22.4	-4.3

na = not available

Source: Yearbook of American and Canadian Churches

[a] includes all clergy, including retired
[b] includes only active clergy serving in churches
[c] 1954 data
[d] 1966 data

Table 4 Distribution of Clergy by Type of Position,
Selected Denominations and Years
(Percentages in Parentheses)

	Parish	Nonparish Ministry	Undesignated or Secular Occupation	Retired	Total
Church of the Nazarene					
1965	4968 (59.9)	1015 (12.3)	1741 (21.0)	566 (6.8)	8290 (100.0)
1970	5073 (55.3)	2044 (22.3)	1329 (14.6)	722 (7.8)	9168 (100.0)
1975	5363 (52.8)	1464 (14.4)	2142 (21.1)	1189 (11.7)	10158 (100.0)
% change 1965-75	+7.9	+44.2	+23.0	+110.0	+22.5
Disciples of Christ					
1950	3820 (57.9)	1011 (15.3)	1146 (17.4)	623 (9.4)	6600 (100.0)
1955	4033 (61.2)	1098 (16.7)	874 (13.3)	580 (8.8)	6585 (100.0)
1960	4244 (62.5)	1132 (16.7)	704 (10.3)	710 (10.5)	6790 (100.0)
1965	3871 (56.6)	1145 (16.7)	742 (10.9)	1080 (15.8)	6838 (100.0)
1970	3114 (48.8)	1190 (18.6)	949 (14.9)	1131 (17.7)	6384 (100.0)
1975	2842 (45.7)	1260 (20.2)	826 (13.3)	1295 (20.8)	6223 (100.0)
% change 1950-75	-25.6	+24.6	-27.9	+207.9	-5.7
Episcopal Church					
1966	7697 (69.2)	1640 (14.8)	599 (5.4)	1179 (10.6)	10801 (100.0)
1970	7295 (61.0)	1784 (14.9)	1436 (12.0)	1448 (12.1)	12079 (100.0)
1974	7670 (59.7)	1774 (13.8)	1652 (12.9)	1741 (13.6)	12837 (100.0)
% change 1966-74	-0.4	+8.1	+175.8	+47.7	+18.9
Presbyterian Church, U.S.					
1965	2744 (65.9)	645 (15.5)	247 (5.9)	528 (12.7)	4164 (100.0)
1970	2791 (60.7)	840 (18.3)	325 (7.1)	639 (13.9)	4595 (100.0)
1975	2818 (55.7)	874 (17.3)	500 (9.9)	867 (17.1)	5059 (100.0)
% change 1965-75	+2.7	+35.5	+102.4	+64.2	+21.5

158

Table 4 Distribution of Clergy by Type of Position,
Selected Denominations and Years
(Percentages in Parentheses)
(continued)

	Parish	Nonparish Ministry	Undesignated or Secular Occupation	Retired	Total
Reformed Church in America					
1967	856	179	10	184	1229
	(69.6)	(14.6)	(0.8)	(15.0)	(100.0)
1976	848	207	56	231	1342
	(63.2)	(15.4)	(4.2)	(17.2)	(100.0)
% change 1967-76	-0.9	+15.6	+460.0	+25.5	+9.2
United Church of Christ					
1966	5571	1476	601	1481	9129
	(61.0)	(16.2)	(6.6)	(16.2)	(100.0)
1971	5123	2629	846	1544	9296
	(55.1)	(28.2)	(9.1)	(16.6)	(100.0)
1976	5031	1809	990	1752	9592
	(52.4)	(19.0)	(10.3)	(18.3)	(100.0)
% change 1966-76	-9.7	+22.6	+64.7	+18.3	+5.1
United Methodist Church					
1960	17415	2510	1663	6260	27848
	(62.5)	(9.0)	(6.0)	(22.5)	(100.0)
1970	21433	4025	2367	6736	34561
	(62.0)	(11.6)	(6.9)	(19.5)	(100.0)
1973	20752	3822	3073	7238	34885
	(59.5)	(11.0)	(8.8)	(20.7)	(100.0)
% change 1960-73	+19.2	+52.2	+84.7	+15.6	+25.2
United Presbyterian Church, U.S.A.*					
1951	5352	1800	1050	1271	9473
	(56.5)	(19.0)	(11.1)	(13.4)	(100.0)
1956	6089	1998	861	1375	10323
	(59.0)	(19.4)	(8.3)	(13.3)	(100.0)
1961	7273	2360	943	1672	12248
	(59.4)	(19.3)	(7.7)	(13.6)	(100.0)
1966	7429	2750	938	1757	12874
	(57.7)	(21.4)	(7.3)	(13.6)	(100.0)
1971	7331	2901	1279	2006	13517
	(54.2)	(21.5)	(9.5)	(14.8)	(100.0)
1976	7330	2765	1324	2427	13846
	(52.9)	(20.0)	(9.6)	(17.5)	(100.0)
% change 1951-76	+37.0	+53.6	+26.1	+91.0	+46.2

*Parish category includes stated supplies

159

Table 5   Distribution of Clergy by Position, 1951-76
The United Presbyterian Church in the U.S.A.
(Percentages in Parentheses)

Year	Pastor	Assoc. Asst. Pastor	Stated Supply	Chap.	Misc.	Educ.	Miss.	Sec'y/ Exec.	Undesig.	Honor. Ret.	Total
1951	4579 (48.3)	278 (3.0)	495 (5.2)	227 (2.4)	225 (2.4)	500 (5.3)	362 (3.8)	486 (5.1)	1050 (11.2)	1271 (13.4)	9473 (100.0)
1956	5006 (48.5)	634 (6.1)	449 (4.3)	273 (2.7)	292 (2.8)	512 (5.0)	356 (3.4)	565 (5.5)	861 (8.3)	1375 (13.4)	10323 (100.0)
1961	5948 (48.6)	997 (8.1)	328 (2.7)	337 (2.7)	310 (2.5)	669 (5.5)	422 (3.4)	622 (5.0)	943 (7.7)	1672 (13.6)	12248 (100.0)
1966	5855 (45.5)	1244 (9.7)	330 (2.6)	419 (3.3)	397 (3.1)	791 (6.2)	399 (3.1)	744 (5.8)	938 (7.3)	1757 (13.6)	12874 (100.0)
1971	5760 (42.6)	1180 (8.7)	391 (2.9)	526 (3.9)	633 (4.7)	939 (6.9)	175 (1.3)	628 (4.6)	1279 (9.5)	2006 (14.8)	13517 (100.0)
1976	5711 (41.2)	1138 (8.2)	481 (3.5)	583 (4.2)	585 (4.2)	890 (6.4)	151 (1.1)	556 (4.0)	1324 (9.6)	2427 (17.5)	13846 (100.0)

Sources: William H. Henderson, "The Professional Ministry of the United Presbyterian Church -- 1975,"
unpublished paper; Comparative Statistics, 1976, The United Presbyterian Church in the U.S.A.

Pastor = pastor, co-pastor, pastor elect, organizing pastor or stated clerk
Chaplain = institutional or military chaplain, university or campus pastor
Miscellaneous = student, evangelist, in transitu, editor, temporary supply, pastor-at-large, librarian,
        field director, field representative or field secretary
Missionary = national or foreign missionary, fraternal worker
Secretary/Executive = secretary (various organizations), counselor, administrator; presbytery executive or
        presbytery staff; synod executive or synod staff; office of the General Assembly,
        General Assembly agencies and councils staff
Honorably Retired = retired, honorably retired, or pastor emeritus

Table 6 Number of Students Completing B.D., M.Div., and (In-Sequence) D.Min. Degrees by Denominational Affiliation of Seminaries, 1969-79*

	1969	1970	1971	1972	1973	1974	1975	1976	1977	1978	1979
American Baptist Churches	228	248	159	150	136	117	131	133	131	136	148
Disciples of Christ	105	106	74	97	91	83	82	86	98	124	103
Episcopal Church	263	271	224	212	234	193	193	207	242	213	236
Lutheran Church in America	na	na	130	208	257	208	199	209	183	204	248
Presbyterian Church, U.S.	105	81	98	78	82	67	53	69	102	100	117
Southern Baptist Convention	517	617	624	637	733	703	693	761	823	993	1040
United Church of Christ	114	99	147	174	155	188	146	154	178	165	215
United Methodist Church	516	676	645	650	656	675	620	663	697	827	757
United Presbyterian Church, U.S.A.	304	294	316	362	308	315	309	235	322	351	337
Inter- or nondenominational	500	561	602	607	618	611	719	860	787	960	1012

na = not available

Source: Factbook on Theological Education, 1969-80 (Vandalia, Ohio: Association of Theological Schools)

*Figures for 1973-76 do not include D.Min. (in-sequence) graduates and therefore underrepresent the actual number of graduates who are candidates for ministry in several denominations, notably Presbyterian U.S. and United Methodist.

Table 7   Women and Black M.Div. Students
as Percentage of Total M.Div. Students
in Seminaries of Selected Denominations, 1976-77

	Women as % of Total	Blacks as % of Total
American Baptist Churches	17.6	16.0
Disciples of Christ	17.2	3.7
Episcopal Church	18.4	2.1
Lutheran Church in America	16.0	1.5
Presbyterian Church, U.S.	15.7	0.9
Southern Baptist Convention	4.4	1.2
United Church of Christ	35.0	4.6
United Methodist Church	21.4	6.4
United Presbyterian, U.S.A.	25.1	4.4
Inter- or nondenominational	14.2	9.1

Source: Factbook on Theological Education, 1976-77
(Vandalia, Ohio: Association of Theological
Schools)

Table 8 Index of Congregational Viability Based on Clergy Salary, Local Program Expenditures, and Per Capita Giving Medians In 1973[a]

	Salary (dollars)			Local Program (dollars)			Per Capita Giving (dollars)			Viability Index (# of members)		
	L	M	U	L	M	U	L	M	U	L	M	U
American Baptist Churches	8970	9900	11225	9200	18800	40855	98	108	117	185	266	445
Church of God (Anderson)	6300	7675	9405	5175	12545	26897	167	200	250	69	101	145
Disciples of Christ	9698	10295	11220	10300	19720	45800	97	100	103	206	300	553
Episcopal Church	12490	13542	14685	12400	27210	60445	125	128	133	199	318	565
Lutheran Church in America	10800	11785	12825	9065	18805	40355	81	91	102	195	336	521
Presbyterian Church, U.S.	10705	11615	14005	8205	20245	63275	119	125	132	159	255	585
Southern Baptist Convention	7096	9605	12550	9000	26100	80700	74	96	117	218	272	797
United Church of Christ[b]	10200	10945	12915	6796	12302	29785	73	80	88	233	291	485
United Methodist Church	9703	11098	12850	7520	16300	40400	62	73	84	278	375	634

L = Median of the lower 50%

M = Median of the total

U = Median of the upper 50%

[a]Data Sources: 1973 Clergy Support Survey

[b]The program totals for UCC seem low and may reflect an error in the data

163

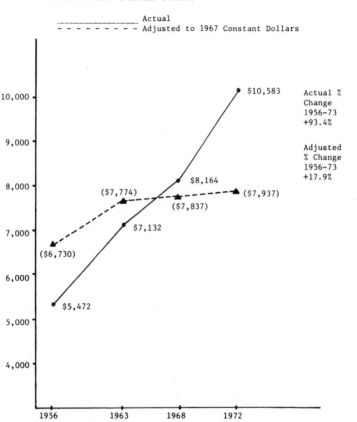

Figure 1   Median Income of Clergy, 1956–73, Actual and Adjusted
Income to 1967 Constant Dollars

————————— Actual
– – – – – – – – – Adjusted to 1967 Constant Dollars

Actual %
Change
1956–73
+93.4%

Adjusted
% Change
1956–73
+17.9%

$10,583

$8,164

($7,774)

($7,937)

($7,837)

$7,132

($6,730)

$5,472

10,000

9,000

8,000

7,000

6,000

5,000

4,000

1956   1963   1968   1972

Sources: F. Ernest Johnson and J. Emory Ackerman, The Church as
Employer, Money Raiser and Investor (New York: Harper & Row, 1959),
p. 149; Ross P. Scherer, "Income and Business Costs of the Protestant
Clergy in 1963," Information Service, vol. 48 (Dec. 5, 1964); Edgar W.
Mills and Janet F. Morse, "Clergy Support in 1968, Incomes and Attitudes,"   Spectrum/Journal, vol. 46 (Jan./Feb., 1970); Robert L. Bonn
and Sheila M. Kelly, "Clergy Support-1973, Salary, Income, and Attitudes," Professional Church Leadership, National Council of Churches, 1974.

164

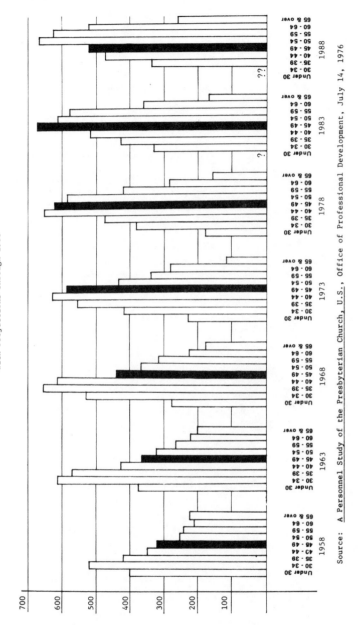

Figure 2 Number of Presbyterian Church, U.S. Ministers in Various Age Categories, in Five-year Intervals, 1958-73, with Projections Through 1988

Source: A Personnel Study of the Presbyterian Church, U.S., Office of Professional Development, July 14, 1976

165

Notes

Foreword

1. William Young Jr., *God's Messengers* (Baltimore: Johns Hopkins Press, 1976), p. 143.

2. An extremely provocative analysis of the impact of careerism can be found in Richard A. Gabriel and Paul L. Savage, *Crisis in Command* (New York: Hill & Wang, 1978), especially pp. 85-115.

Introduction

1. Jackson W. Carroll and Robert L. Wilson, *The Clergy Job Market: Oversupply and/or Opportunity* (Hartford, Conn.: Hartford Seminary Foundation, 1978).

Chapter 2 More Called Than Chosen

1. In computing the ratios we used the figure for total clergy, which includes retired clergy as well as active clergy serving in parish and nonparish positions. While the inclusion of retired clergy somewhat inflates the number of clergy, we have no way of separating them out from the rest. There are, however, many officially retired clergy who continue to serve churches part or full time. Thus the distortion of the ratios is not likely to be serious.

2. Gibson Winter, *Religious Identity* (New York: Macmillan, 1968), p. 123.

3. The data summarized in Table 4 is from those denominations for which time series breakdowns of clergy in various types of positions were available. Data was not available for the same years for all denominations. Because denominations use differing categories for classifying clergy, we have reclassified the data into uniform categories to allow for comparability between denominations. Table 5 shows time series data from 1951 through 1976 for the United Presbyterians, to illustrate detailed changes in types of

ministry positions over a twenty-five-year period that are less evident in the time series available from most other denominations.

4. The Association of Theological Schools did not differentiate between types of degrees in their annual reports until 1969. Between 1969 and 1977 there has been a 20 percent increase in B.D. and M.Div. enrollments.

5. Edward C. Lehman, Jr., "Sex-Linked Patterns of Placement in the Ministry," unpublished paper, 1979.

6. While all the denominations have a wide diversity of types of churches that have differing expectations for pastoral leadership, this is especially true for Southern Baptists. In an unpublished paper presented at the annual meeting of the Religious Research Association in 1977, William Garrett used naval terminology to delineate the types: the *PT Boat* (small, rural, fundamentalist, usually with a bivocational minister); the *Destroyer* (churches in small towns and on the urban fringe); the *Cruiser* (affluent, middle class, suburban); and the *Battleship* (the large, downtown First Baptist Church). Such diversity makes it virtually impossible to generalize about the supply and demand for clergy in the Southern Baptist Convention.

7. J. Clifford Tharp, Jr., "Paid Professional Staff Personnel of Southern Baptist Churches and Association," *The Quarterly Review,* vol. 36 (Jan.-Feb.-March 1976), pp. 36-56.

8. "Survey of Various Denominations Regarding Their Supply of Pastors." North American Baptist Conference, Forest Park, Illinois, February 24, 1976. We are indebted to the Rev. John Binder for sharing the survey with us.

9. "Replacing a Lost Generation of Leaders," United Church of Christ Sunday Bulletin Service, September 19, 1976.

Chapter 3 Why So Many Ordained Ministers?

1. Helen Axel, ed., *A Guide to Consumer Markets 1975/1976* (New York: The Conference Board, 1975), pp. 16, 18.

2. Alexander W. Astin, *The American Freshman: National Norms for Fall* (Cooperative Institutional Research Program, American Council on Education and University of California at Los Angeles, 1968-75).

3. Richard B. Freeman, *The Over-Educated American* (New York: Academic Press, 1976), p. 79.

4. Jackson W. Carroll and Robert L. Wilson, *The Clergy Job Market, Oversupply and/or Opportunity* (Hartford, Conn.: Hartford Seminary Foundation, 1978), p. 90.

5. Freeman, *The Over-Educated American,* op. cit., pp. 175-79. See also Allan Carter, *Ph.D.'s and the Academic Labor Market* (New York: McGraw-Hill, 1976), pp. 51-53.

6. Jeremy Main, "Careers in the 1980s: 10 of the Best and 10 of the Worst," *Money,* November 1977, p. 64.

7. Hubert Herring, "The Minister and the Depression," *The Nation,* vol. 138 (January 17, 1934), p. 66.

8. *Minutes of the General Assembly of the United Presbyterian Church of North America,* vol. 18 (1932), p. 41.

9. "Depression in the Pulpit," *The Literary Digest,* vol. 111 (December 10, 1931), p. 19.

10. *Minutes of the General Assembly of the United Presbyterian Church of North America,* vol. 19 (1939), p. 1080.

11. Nathan H. Vanderwerf, *The Times Were Very Full* (New York: National Council of Churches of Christ in the U.S.A., 1975), p. 39.

Chapter 4 Consequences for the Clergy

1. Cited in Donald P. Smith, "Toward a Strategy for Theological Education," an address to the United Presbyterian Council of Theological Seminaries, November 11, 1976, p. 5 (Xeroxed).

Chapter 5 Sisters in the Brotherhood

1. Constant Jacquet, *Women Ministers 1977* (New York: Office of Research, Evaluation and Planning, National Council of Churches, 1977).

2. Edward C. Lehman, Jr., "Sex-Linked Patterns of Placement in the Ministry," unpublished paper, 1979.

3. For a descriptive case study of such an arrangement, see Elisa DesPortes Wheeler, *Clergy Couple, A Case Study of One Couple's Experience in Ministry* (Hartford, Conn.: Hartford Seminary Foundation, 1976). For a more general discussion of clergy couples, see John P. von Lackum, III and Nancy Jo Kemper von Lackum,

Clergy Couples (New York: Professional Church Leadership, National Council of Churches, 1979).

Chapter 7 Rethinking Ordination

1. Marc Connelly, *The Green Pastures, A Fable* (New York: Farrar & Rinehart, 1929), p. 69.

2. See Bernard Cooke, *Ministry to Word and Sacrament* (Philadelphia: Fortress Press, 1976), p. 91.

3. H. Richard Niebuhr, in *The Purpose of the Church and the Ministry* (New York: Harper & Row, 1956), p. 64, distinguishes four types of call: (1) *the call to be a Christian,* (2) *the secret call,* (3) *the providential call,* and (4) *the ecclesiastical call.*

4. Edward Schweizer, *Church Order in the New Testament* (London: SCM Press, 1961), pp. 194-97.

5. See ibid., pp. 197-205, and John Knox, "The Ministry in the Primitive Church," in H. Richard Niebuhr and Daniel Day Williams, eds., *The Ministry in Historical Perspectives* (New York: Harper & Row, 1956), pp. 1-26.

6. See Knox, "The Ministry in the Primitive Church," op. cit.; pp. 23-25.

7. Cooke, *Ministry to Word and Sacrament,* op. cit., p. 266.

8. Graham Greene, *The Power and the Glory* (New York: Viking Press, 1940), p. 263.

9. George H. Williams, "The Ministry in the Later Patristic Period (314-451)," in H. Richard Niebuhr and Daniel Day Williams, eds., *The Ministry in Historical Perspectives* (New York: Harper & Row, 1956), p. 75.

10. Gerald J. Jud, Edgar W. Mills, Jr., and Genevieve W. Burch, *Ex Pastors* (Philadelphia: Pilgrim Press, 1970), p. 54.

11. Knox, "The Ministry in the Primitive Church," op. cit., p. 25.

12. George H. Williams, "The Ministry of the Ante-Nicene Church (c. 125-325)," Niebuhr and Williams, eds., *The Ministry in Historical Perspectives,* op. cit., pp. 28-29.

13. See Niebuhr, *The Purpose of the Church and the Ministry,* op. cit., pp. 58ff.

14. See Hans Küng, *On Being a Christian,* trans. by Edward Quinn (Garden City, N.Y.: Doubleday, 1976), p. 493. Küng assumes that

proclamation and administration of the sacraments are the main task of the mission of Christ for which ordination gives authority.

Chapter 8 Survival Tactics for Clergy

1. See Mark A. Rouch, *Young Pastors* (Nashville: United Methodist Division of the Ordained Ministry, 1973) for a report of a pilot project for young pastors. The United Presbyterian Vocations Agency has proposed an ambitious program, "Introduction to Ministry," in which judicatories, seminaries, career counseling centers, families, and so on will be involved in a program for young clergy. The Hartford Seminary Foundation offers a "Year of Renewal for Clergy," a program designed especially for clergy in midcareer.

2. Robert L. Bonn, *Continuing Education Participants: Who, How Many, Types of Program* (Richmond, Va.: Society for the Advancement of Continuing Education for Ministry, 1975).

3. John C. Fletcher, *Religious Authenticity in the Clergy* (Washington: Alban Institute, 1975), p. 1.

4. One of the best is Richard Nelson Bolles, *What Color is Your Parachute?* (Berkeley, Calif: Ten Speed Press, 1979).

5. John C. Harris, *Stress, Power and Ministry* (Washington: Alban Institute, 1977), p. 163.

Chapter 9 Cassocks and Coveralls

1. James L. Lowery, Jr., ed., *Case Histories of Tentmakers* (Wilton, Conn., 1976), p. 76.

2. Robert L. Bonn, "Moonlighting Clergy," *The Christian Ministry,* September 1975, pp. 4-8.

3. Ruth Doyle and Sheila Kelly, "Distribution and Deployment of Clergy in The Episcopal Church, 1970-1974" (New York: Clergy Deployment Office of The Episcopal Church, n.d.).

4. Clay Price, "A Brief Comparison of Small Rural Churches with Bi-Vocational Pastors to Small Rural Churches with Full-Time Pastors" (Southern Baptist Convention Mission Surveys and Special Studies, 1977), Xeroxed paper.

5. Bonn, "Moonlighting Clergy," op. cit., p. 4.

6. Lowery, *Case Histories of Tentmakers,* op. cit., p. 78.

7. Bonn, "Moonlighting Clergy," op. cit., pp. 5, 7.

8. Jackson W. Carroll and Robert L. Wilson, *The Clergy Job*

Market, Oversupply and/or Opportunity (Hartford, Conn.: Hartford Seminary Foundation, 1978), p. 92.

9. Quoted in George Vecsey, "Clergy Turn to Other Work to Supplement the Lord's," *The New York Times,* December 26, 1978.

10. See Robert L. Bonn and Ruth T. Doyle, "Secularly Employed Clergymen: A Study in Occupational Role Recomposition," *Journal for the Scientific Study of Religion,* vol. 13 (September 1974), pp. 335-36.

11. Paul Andrews, "The Sacramental Color of a Fire Engine," *The Christian Century,* June 1, 1977, p. 550.

12. *Dual-Role Pastorate, The Explorations and Learnings of CODE, Clergy Occupational Development and Employment Project, 1975-1978* (Rochester, N.Y.: CODE, 1978), Xeroxed report. We are particularly grateful to Dorothy Greenwood, CODE Director, and the CODE Management Committee for sharing with us so generously of their time and insights during several visits to the CODE project.

Chapter 10 The Church System and Clergy Employment

1. Several helpful research reports and guidebooks have been written that deal with the vacancy experience. See, for example, Celia A. Hahn, *The Minister Is Leaving* (New York: Seabury Press); Loyde H. Hartley, *Pastoral Search Committees* (Lancaster, Pa.: Research Center in Religion and Society, 1975); and David C. Eaton, "A Nominating Committee Chairman Reports on One Congregation's Experience in Calling a New Pastor," First Presbyterian Church, Normal, Illinois, 1973 (mimeographed).

2. George L. Garver, "Concerning the 'Surplus of Clergy' and Outplacement of Pastors in the LCA," mimeographed paper, n.d.

3. A seminary that has developed a program to meet both of these needs is The School of Theology of the University of the South (Episcopal) in its four-year program of Theological Education by Extension. It uses seminary-prepared materials and mentors who meet with small groups of laity to facilitate discussion of the materials.